Love and Laughter

by

MARJORIE HOLMES

Garden City, New York
DOUBLEDAY & COMPANY, INC.

Library of Congress Catalog Card Number 67-11178
Copyright © 1959, 1967 by Marjorie Holmes Mighell
All Rights Reserved
Printed in the United States of America

For
 Mickie,
  Mark,
   Mallory,
    Melanie,
     and Lynn.

FOREWORD

THIS BOOK is in response to the many requests that have been received from readers of the column, "Love and Laughter," that appears in the Washington *Evening Star*. The author wishes to thank the publishers of the *Star* for permission to reprint these sketches in book form. Thanks are also extended to *McCall's* magazine, *Better Homes & Gardens, American Home, Today's Health, Guideposts, Everywoman's Family Circle,* and *Reader's Digest* for permission to include other sketches which first appeared in their pages.

Contents

A Woman and Her Home

I have my own home, to do what I please with, to do
what I please with. My den for me and my mate and
my cubs, my own!

— *Song of the ancient gods*
of the hearth

HER ARK AND HER COVENANT

IT HAS BEEN SAID of man that his home is his castle. But what of woman? Strangely, few phrases have been coined to express the significance of home to her, the person who presides over its every function. What, then, is home to a woman?

Often, to be quite honest, home represents chaos, confusion, and quarrels. It is a place so hectic that sometimes, if we are human, we long only to escape. Time and again women, good women, have said to me, "I reach a point where I actually have insane thoughts of running off. Just any place to get away!"

A great deal of the time home to a woman is just plain old-fashioned work. Meals and dishes and ironing curtains and cleaning the closets and washing clothes.

Frequently it is entertaining. Everything slick and shining, and heavenly smells from the oven, and counting the silver, and baths early for everybody so that fresh towels can be up. And flowers and mints and nuts, and the sheer delight of pleasant voices exclaiming, "My, what a beautiful home."

A lot of the time it's worry—four walls that hold more concentrated concern than it seems any soul can bear: Will your son pass? Is your daughter really serious about that impossible boy she insists on seeing? Why can't the doctors find out what's wrong with John? Why doesn't money go further? How will the budget stand the added strain of college?

A great deal of the time it's fun. Small fry prancing about, so comically sweet in their antics you must scoop them into your arms. Teen-agers doing card tricks, dancing, playing the piano. Neighbors popping in for coffee. Your husband cornering you in the kitchen to tell you that funny story he heard at his luncheon club.

Her home is all these things to a woman, and a whole lot more.

Something intangible. Something deeper. Something impossible to capture in a phrase.

Home is both the place where she is sheltered from the world, yet where her weaknesses and failures are exposed. Both the prison from which she cannot escape, yet the place where she is freest.

And here, for all its turbulence and burdens, she is its keynote. The touchstone for other people's progress. The focal point from which the spokes of their lives radiate.

As such, her home is not a matter of rugs and linens and beds and the washing machine and the kitchen stove. It is not the walls that surround it nor the contents of its rooms. It is both an ark—and a covenant.

Her ark for her protection. Her covenant with the future. It is her destiny.

IT'S NOT THE DIRT, IT'S THE DISORDER

IT ISN'T THE DIRT that gets most housewives down so much as it is the disorder. The incessant need for picking up after people. The constant coping with clutter.

It's the hanging up of coats and scarves that are shed on the bench in the hall. It's the putting away of gloves and purses and boots and patrol belts. It's the trotting to the toy cupboards with armloads of dolls and bears and jacks and pieces of jigsaw puzzles.

It's the insoluble daily dilemma over what to do with school papers and drawings and *Junior Scholastic*. It's the eternal hassle with magazines. No matter how conscientiously you assemble them into their proper piles, *National Geographic* invariably goes traveling. *The Saturday Evening Post* gets mixed up with *Life* and *Popular Mechanics*. *Reader's Digest* romps merrily with *McCall's*, and *Esquire* and *Guideposts* get gaily if incongruously together.

As for those brashly ambitious attempts to stack them not only with their proper families, but according to months—what folly! Last year's Christmas issue is bound to bounce to the top in July.

Bathrooms are another place guaranteed to break a tidy housewife's heart. No sooner do you get the towels neatly folded on their bars than flop—they're on the floor. Gleaming basins become grubby puddles before the day is advanced by a few hours. Toothbrushes seldom find their way back to their proper holders. And twisted, tortured toothpaste tubes ooze at you, always minus caps.

Then there is the sheer, cussed, incomprehensible enemy—things lying on top of things. How, oh how does anybody keep the surfaces of tables, buffets, dressers tidy and shiny when an army of miscellany invades them hour by hour and fiercely holds the fort? Mail, trading stamps, pencils, homework, bobby pins, thumbtacks, bits and pieces of broken items—a screw from this, a handle, arm, eye, knob, nail, propeller or feather from that.

You gather them up onto your person; your pockets bulge with them. Trudge, trudge, trudge, you go about trying to find the origin of all these items, to lead them safely home and maybe by locking doors or slamming drawers, keep them at bay. Yet by some evil cunning they have reappeared before you can scarcely turn your back. This sometimes happens even when there's nobody else in the house. They seem to descend from the ceiling, or emerge slyly out of cracks.

"Train your children to be neat," we are advised—and this too is a part of the very problem. How is it possible to achieve and maintain order in a family without becoming a mean old witch? "Don't yell at your children," we are also warned. But how else are you going to get Jimmy to pick up his ball bat, hang up his pajamas, make his bed, feed and clean up after his pets, and at the same time make himself presentable and on time to catch the school bus?

If you don't holler nobody listens. If you do ride herd, well—you're also the one that rides the broomstick!

WAYS TO OUTWIT THE IRONING

WHAT A PLEASURE it is to finish the ironing—really finish it, down to the last pesky dresser scarf, hanky, and whatsit in the basket. To gaze upon the neat stacks and hangers and foldings of your accomplishment. To think, "Well, for a week at least, the ironing's done."

Ironing has a built-in tendency to multiply and mount. It's so easy to toss a bunch of clothes into the washer and dryer; but such a monumental effort to overcome the barrier that keeps you from getting them wearably back to closets and drawers.

"My ironing resembles a mountain," a neighbor said the other day. "Whenever it threatens to touch the ceiling, I just snatch off the top and iron it." This is true of a lot of us. Or when somebody yells, "I've got to have a shirt," or, "I can't find a decent clean pair of slacks," you dash for the board and get them pressed somehow.

My favorite crack from comedienne Phyllis Diller is—"I'm eighteen years behind on my ironing. There's no use doing it now, it doesn't fit anybody I know!"

Ironing is the primary reason most women hire day help. It's the one job most of us dread. Yet ironing isn't so bad once you get at it, tackle it as if you mean business, and stick to it. And there are ways to simplify and outwit it.

For one thing, if you have a steam iron and a shaker you don't have to go through the long waste motion of dampening. Just steam and sprinkle as you proceed. Or use spray starch. Also, if you wait until after dinner you can iron and yell at people and supervise homework and more or less watch TV at one fell scorch. This diversifying of your attention keeps the job from seeming too much the master, you the slave.

Another good idea is to mend things as you iron them. With button box and sewing machine close by, you can send a blouse back to its owner with all buttons intact, and suture trouser slits. Thus you won't have to start dreading the *mending* once you get the ironing licked.

Another nice thing about *not* having a maid to iron for you is that inevitably a stranger will mix up everybody's belongings so that morning can be a madhouse with people flying from room to room and wrestling through drawers trying to find their own slips or socks.

Yes, indeedy, ironing can be just jim-dandy. Now hand me the classifieds, somebody; tell me a good employment agency. Help! Wanted: Somebody to do the ironing!

CURTAINS

CURTAINS . . . An armful of ruffled white organdy. A length of lace. Or a thick, lined oblong of material to draw against the dark.

How much of a woman's life is devoted to these innocent-looking tyrants. How many hours in the selecting or making thereof. In the arduous if challenging business of hanging them up and taking them down. In the washing and ironing.

"Did the first people have curtains at their windows?" your little boy asks as you sit whipping up a new set at the sewing machine.

"No. The first people lived in caves with holes in the top to let out the smoke." (Lucky cave women, you think.) "They didn't have windows. The pioneers had windows in their cabins, but sometimes they didn't have glass to keep out the cold. They used paper, I believe I read somewhere."

"Funny papers? Hey, that'd be great."

"No, this was long before comic strips." You shake out the rectangle of ruffled print you are working on. "And I'm sure very few of them actually had curtains until later on."

"Were they too busy making soap and chasing the Indians off?"

"I guess, probably," you laugh. "And I doubt if it was easy to get the material. It was many miles to the nearest store. Most of the material they had, even for clothes, they had to weave themselves. (Come to think of it, you'd rather cope with curtains.) "No, I don't imagine pretty curtains at the windows were a very common sight."

"If they got along without curtains, why don't we?" he reasons, lounging on the sill. With a finger, he begins to write his name on the dusty glass.

"Dear, don't do that."

"Why not? They're dirty, anyway."

"That gives me an idea—you can wash them."

"Oh, boy, can I?" He's still young enough to greet this with rejoicing. With gusto he smears the cleaner and begins boldly to letter his name on that.

"We hang curtains, I guess, because we're used to them," you tell him. "A house looks sort of undressed without its curtains up." And this is true. You recall all the places you have lived, and your parents before you, and those of other people; and how there is always this sense of echoing emptiness until those snug squares are safely in place.

"Also, curtains give us a sense of privacy, so that other people can't see in."

"I *like* to see in. I like going along the street where they have big picture windows and you can see the lamps and the people and what they're doing. Makes it interesting."

"I like to too," you agree. "It's like catching a glimpse of a play on a stage. But they still have draperies, usually, that they can pull when they want."

You snip the final thread, reach for a rod. Anticipation begins to mount as you work the rod through. Nothing like new curtains to brighten up a room. "How'd you like to help me hang them?" you ask. "You may as well learn. You'll be doing it for your wife some day."

THE DINNER HOUR

IT HAPPENS in almost every house:

At the tender behest of husband and kiddies, Mother takes a well-earned vacation at the home of a cultured, well-to-do, and incidentally childless, girlhood friend.

She returns home not only soothed in body and spirit, but inspired. Meals, for instance. Now there's simply no reason why ours have to be so hectic. Dinner, especially, she thinks. It doesn't take money to achieve an atmosphere of charm and quiet. It merely takes time, efficient management, and the little artistic touches of a woman who simply *cares* enough.

So instead of the more probable pot roast, she lavishes the afternoon on a seafood casserole, replete with herbs and cheese and wine. She crisps up a big green salad, and decides it might even be amusing to start off with little cups of vichyssoise.

As the dinner hour approaches, she interrupts the operations of three vigorously dissenting kite builders on the dining room table, and patiently polishes same. She arranges sprigs of ivy and laurel into a reasonable facsimile of a centerpiece. She gets out the candlesticks.

"Oh, boy, company! Who's coming?" the shout goes up.

"Nobody's coming, but we're all going to *act* like company," she explains. "No arguing, no elbows on the table, just good conversation and good food, with some good music in the background to put us all in the mood."

With an air of sweet resolution, she selects a symphony for the record player. Just a little planning, that's all it takes. Just the props and arrangements of beauty and grace.

But the first fight erupts as she's dishing up. "I get to light the candles." . . . "No, me, no, me!" There is a frantic scrambling, a shoving for position, followed by shouts of anger as somebody blows them out and somebody else burns a finger and goes howling to the bathroom for first aid.

The father, meanwhile, demands, "Why all the ruckus, and why all the dark?" and flicks the overhead lights on.

Oh, well, the candles will still be nice, the mother thinks, lighting them herself and making everybody sit down. And she can't help feeling a proud little thrill over the vichyssoise.

"What's this stuff?" one boy demands, skeptically sniffing.

"A French potato soup. Now eat it, you'll love it." She glances appealingly at her husband, who loyally orders, "That's right, if your mother made it you eat it, whether you like it or not."

This wasn't exactly the reaction she'd anticipated, but no matter. And when the first cup is spilled, and in chain reaction, two more, at least it's a relief from the usual milk. At least if they've got to spill something it's more refined to spill vichyssoise.

The symphony! My goodness, she forgot to put on the symphony, she realizes, leaping up to attend to it, while others dash to the kitchen for sponges, towels, and to summon the dog. Brahms, that's what they needed, a good soothing background of Brahms.

"Turn that thing down," somebody yells as she returns, "I'm on the phone!" The doorbell is ringing. Elbows are on the table and arguments are going strong. The dog provides an efficient but inartistic touch, slurping up the spilled vichyssoise.

She is home.

THE PEOPLE WHO USED TO
LIVE HERE

HAVE YOU EVER FELT that sometimes when you buy a house you buy a family with it?

It may be the family that has just packed up and is departing as you (feeling a bit shy and strange, almost the apologetic intruder) move your own crew in. For a little while the ghosts of this former family linger. You find them popping out at you from closets and cupboards—in a sash from a little red dress that still dangles on a hook, a garden hat, a book, a sheaf of accounts, a forgotten toy.

The personality of your predecessor seems to be watching as you get acquainted with her sink, her stove, hang curtains at what were once her windows. "No, no, not that way, stupid," you nervously fancy her scolding. And unconsciously defend, "Look, it's *my* house now, and you'll be surprised at the improvements I'll make."

Then you laugh at your own absurdity—feeling rivals, imagine! —and something warm and nice comes over you as you see that she's left a casserole in the refrigerator, a list of baby sitters, and those bedroom draperies you admired.

In most cases they leave rather quickly, these forerunners who lived here. They fade, they vanish, you forget that this roof and these walls ever sheltered anyone else. No matter how often the neighbors refer to them, or how many preceded you, there is the conviction that this house now firmly and forever has been yours.

Yet in an old house this is not always the case. A very old house that another family built long ago when the neighborhood was new, and lived in fully and richly until they went their separate ways and the house fell into impersonal hands. And though we have lived here twelve years now, I sometimes wonder if the huge old house we occupy will ever fully and completely belong to us? For they were waiting for us in the attic the day we came, those gracious ladies and gentlemen of the past.

They smiled at us from their photographs. And when we plunged into ancient trunks that had obviously been many times around the world, we found even more graphic evidence—for there, enchantingly, were their bustles and bonnets and high-button shoes and tall silk hats.

Many of their letters they left behind them too. Invitations and bits of small talk written in fine and elegant script. Magic lantern slides taken in Egypt, the Philippines, Japan. Diplomas. Citations.

And though they have all been gone for many years now, neighbors—old neighbors who knew them at the height of their prominence, still speak of them. And their words are filled with admiration and affection. "Oh, yes, everybody knew the Corbetts." And people still refer to the house where we live as "The Corbett House."

And one day, to our joy and amazement, some of them, living people, not ghosts at all, but vivid young descendants, came swarming in. And expressed astonishment and delight that we had actually saved some of those souvenirs of their ancestral past.

"Well, we just couldn't bear to throw them out," we admitted. "After building the house and living in it so many years—well, it sort of seemed as if your family, as well as its house, belonged to us."

LONG LOST FRIENDS

IT HAPPENS in almost every house:

The phone rings and you hear the voice of some friend, relative (or friend of a friend or relative) so long lost you grope to place the identity. "Why—why, how wonderful," you exclaim. "Where *are* you?"

And as they admit they are either in the city or approaching it, "Gracious, we'd just love to see you—" even as you make frantic calculations: How many beds can we make up? Did those towels get back from the laundry? "You—you must come out for dinner." And as they demur that they wouldn't want to put you to any trouble, you not only insist, you find yourself urging that they spend the night. No, no, it won't put you out a bit, you won't do a *thing*.

Hanging up, you gaze wildly about the tumbled house. And food! You can hardly feed them the intended leftovers and it's too late to thaw a roast; you'll have to go to the store. Meanwhile, you start barking orders: "Pat, go clean up your room, they'll have to sleep there—you can have the couch. Freddy, put those puzzles away and sweep the rug. Janey, go out in the yard with Jimmy and see if you can find enough dry branches to start a fire. Also, anything that remotely resembles flowers. Now *hurry*, everybody, they should be here in an hour."

And you go galloping off to the grocery intent only on steak for supper, bacon for breakfast, lettuce, some rolls—and spend twenty dollars. And there's a long line before the cashier, it takes longer than you thought; and as you finally come panting into the homestretch, you see, with sinking heart, the out-of-state car.

They've found a shortcut, they announce triumphantly over the kisses and exclamations—here they are!

And the fireplace that should be blazing brightly is stone cold. Janey comes in with three frostbitten, bedraggled weeds. The sweeper's dead center of the rug while Freddy gazes transfixed at the TV set. And why, oh why didn't you at least put on a skirt before going to the store?

But, still frowsy and frenzied, you strive to be the cordial hostess even as you stash some groceries away, snatch out others. And if your husband is going to have all these relatives why can't he get home and help entertain them? And thank goodness here he is to make the fire and mix the drinks and bolster conversation while you get dinner on.

And between courses you slip to the basement to check the sheets and signal a daughter to iron them before the evening's over, hoping she doesn't get the one with the mended place in the middle. And *where* did you put those thick bright Christmas-present towels?

And you sit up late visiting, showing home movies, getting acquainted or reacquainted, and there is a sense of fellowship, of warmth and goodness and drawing together that compensates for the confusion. And when at last you are all bedded down you whisper to your husband, "They're really lovely, aren't they? I'm really glad they came."

And in the morning you linger over a fresh pot of coffee after the children are off to school. You find yourself urging, "You

don't have to go on today, do you? Can't we show you around?"
And when the hearty thanks and farewells have been said, you
wave at the departing car with a curious sense of loss. "Good-by,
good-by, come back soon!" you call—and mean it.

It's been worth all the trouble.

THE FAMILY TABLE

You sit around it together, the antique black walnut table that
your husband bought with a bunch of junk furniture and lovingly
refinished years ago.

It took him months to complete that single project, so carefully did he sand and plane and varnish and wax, until its surface
was smooth as glass and hard as stone. It will take the hottest
dish and survive the roughest blows. The dog has chewed its legs
without much damage; it wasn't too much hurt even when a
chafing dish caught fire once and burned up a tablecloth. Long
and steady it stands there, opening up for additional leaves when
guests are coming, shrinking smaller and smaller as children go
away from home.

How many meals have been served there? you sometimes
wonder, getting down the plates to set it another time. How many
birthday cakes and Thanksgiving turkeys and Christmas dinners
has it known? How many kites have littered its broad expanse,
how many model planes and scrapbooks and doll clothes?

How many bills have been paid there, how many notes written
to teachers, how many income tax forms? For that matter, how
many apples have probably been peeled there, how much canning
done? For it bore the marks of knives and jars and water buckets
when your husband first came carting it home.

And you think back to all those other lives which came to this
selfsame table before you. The women, busy at their humble
kitchen tasks before clearing it, as was often done, to set it for
supper. The men who sat down to carve. And the children, the

many children, excited about their birthday cakes, their Thanksgiving drumsticks, their news about love affairs or school.

People. Living people drawn together at a sturdy table. And you think of the laughter and the tears and the arguments and stormy scenes this table has known. They are its essence, a part of it like its grain. And it is this which gives an antique its true value and meaning. It is old and warm and wise with living. It is like a person who only grows more beautiful with age.

THE BUFFET DRAWER

HERE's to that great repository of American living, the buffet drawer!

Even if you eat at a breakfast nook or a coffee bar in the kitchen, you must pass it, usually, on your countless travels throughout the house. And as you do so it awaits you, silent-mouthed but ever ready to open and gulp the flotsam and jetsam that nobody knows quite what to do with:

The door keys. The Charge-a-Plate. The school papers, the safety pins, the bargain soap coupons. The pencils, the notices, the pamphlets that nobody reads but somebody might want to, so you'd better not throw them out.

What housewife is so equipped with will power that, dizzily viewing the constant accumulation, she doesn't shut her eyes and simply scoop it into the blind relief of the buffet drawer?

What female is so firm in her demands that she can enforce a more orderly disposal of possessions upon her progeny? "These are your ball and jacks, take them to *your own room!*" . . . "This is your party invitation, put it where you can find it, for goodness sake." Thus though we chant in a kind of dutiful recitative day in and day out, who heeds, pray tell? Who obeys?

No, there exists a kind of common understanding: If you don't need it but want to keep it, where more safely can it go on deposit than in the buffet drawer? We even answer all inquiries thus ourselves: "Where can you find some bobby pins? Look in the buffet drawer." . . . "Has anybody seen your Scout knife? It's probably in the buffet drawer."

And even if the missing object isn't at once unearthed, how often other treasures are: "Hey, here's that cowboy wallet Grandma gave me for Christmas two years ago." . . . "I only scared up three bobby pins, but I found this jeweled barrette and this rabbit's foot and it's already brought me luck—look, here's a movie pass and it's not even dated and there's a neat matinee this afternoon."

Betimes, of course, you clean it. When it reaches the point of sheer satiety. When its jaws are so bulging full they're beginning to show leakage and you can scarcely shut them. In a burst of reform you dump the entire contents on the dining room table and sort. The tacks, the lipsticks, the buttons, the jewelry—each in its proper heap to be tidily distributed or filed away in boxes and jars. A lot of the papers can be burned—the notices of a citizens' meeting four months ago, the homework; yea, though you feel guilty twinges, those unredeemed soap coupons.

My heavens, how bare it is. How neatly compartmentalized, you gloat. This section for school tickets and such. This for the circulars. This one for combs. "And there's simply *no excuse* for its getting into such a mess again," you lecture with fervor and hope. In fact it's so clean it intimidates even you. For a little while you actually refrain from the daily sweep yourself.

But soon—just when one cannot say—you too know the sweet relief of its all-embracing vaults. Of answering the inevitable, "What'll I do with this?" by the equally inevitable, "Well, for now—put it in the buffet drawer." And the queries, "Where can I find it?" with that comfortable, dependable prediction: "You know very well where it probably is—the buffet drawer!"

THOSE "VALUABLE COUPONS"

HELP! They arrive in a plain envelope marked "occupant," and though you're tempted to throw them away unopened, you know it's hopeless. The children will only rescue them exclaiming, "Look, Mommy, why look, here's a letter you didn't open."

And they're even more excited when they discover its contents. Bright-hued coupons that sometimes look like money. Slips that proclaim the wonders of soup or soap, margarine or mayonnaise, and what's more will save you ten cents on your next purchase.

So that you realize, "Dear me, that's right, I really ought to take advantage of this." Arousing in you guilt feeling for your rash improvidence if you don't, albeit a kind of resentment at being so insidiously enslaved.

So the next time you go to market you've got to remember to take the darned things along. And oh, dear, where are they? And so many of them, too—how they accumulate.

So instead of poking pleasantly down the aisles selecting what you want or need, you find yourself on a kind of half-amused, half-determined treasure hunt, scouting out the certain brands (often of items you never use and have a sneaking suspicion you never will). Yet once dedicated to this silly mission you feel morally obligated to track down every so-called bargain, from perfumed starch to fluted sandwich bags.

Now there follows some frenetic arithmetic. In addition to all the coupons clutched in your fists, you are further lured by a sign above the scouring powder which announces, "Two for 27 cents." And wait, as if this weren't enough, another sign upon each can joyously proclaims, "Ten cents off!"

With a gush of gratitude for the manufacturer, you reach for the spoils. Two goes into twenty-seven how many times? Well, let's make it roughly fourteen cents a can (fractions always throw you). Hey, and then there's ten cents off. That leaves it four cents apiece; times two makes eight cents—and you're holding a coupon worth ten cents. Why, at this rate you'll come out money ahead!

The cashier dashes your triumph, however. The ten cents off doesn't apply if you're buying two for one, he informs you. Your dime saving coupon applies only to the super-giant size selling for fifty-nine cents. And half the other coupons expired three months ago.

Too exhausted and embarrassed even to consider trekking around putting things back, you haul them home. Only to find further enslavement tucked diabolically inside each package. A spanking new coupon leers at you: "Fifteen cents off!"

"YOUR HOUSE SMELLS SO GOOD"

HOUSES are like the people who live in them. They are a showcase of the kind of things people like to have about them. And subtly yet distinctively they reveal their occupants' nature in the very way they smell.

One of my neighbors' houses has such a clean and housewifey scent. It smells of the ironing she's always doing at odd hours— of the flocks of crisp little dresses and starched white shirts that hang over the backs of chairs. . . . It smells of the baby—its formula, its freshly folded diapers, its talcum, and its toys. . . . It smells of the big brown pot roast simmering in the kitchen, and the just baked cinnamon rolls set out to cool.

Some houses smell of sickness and age and mustiness and death. They are dark and unaired and dismal. Yet the houses of old people need not have this odor.

My own grandparents' home always smelled of apples. There were great bins of them in the basement, brought in from the farm. Grandmother kept a huge blue Chinese bowl of them on the dining room table, and our grandpa, who seemed to us a very old man, a man of great dignity and dominance, with a perky

Uncle Sam goatee, would pare them for us, the peels uncoiling rosily on the thick white linen cloth. . . . The kitchen smelled of gingerbread and sour cream cookies, and the upstairs of sachet.

Kitchen fans have their place and deodorizers too, I guess. But I don't mind home smells, people smells. The smells of bacon frying, or onions, don't offend me in the least. Or the smell of pets. Or the smell of a father's greasy guns and hobbies.

These odors are the breath of living. They are human. They are good.

A Woman and Her Children

I love these little people, and it is not a slight thing when they, who are so fresh from God, love us.

— *Charles Dickens*

CHILDREN'S HANDS

CHILDREN'S HANDS . . .

First they are but tiny tendrils, gripping your finger, brushing at your breast . . .

Next they are plump and dimpled, getting into things so that you must say, "No, no!" continually. Or, "Mustn't touch, naughty hands." . . .

Then, still small and grubby, they are clutching crayons, scribbling. Or groping awkwardly with pencils, learning to print their names . . .

Then soon, so soon, they are lengthening—catching baseballs, swinging ropes for jumping, playing jacks . . .

And a little longer still, anxiously struggling to tie a necktie for a party, or applying a first excited touch of lipstick . . .

And now, longer and stronger yet, they are being fitted for class rings, adjusting the unfamiliar robes and tasseled hats for Commencement, reaching out to take diplomas from older, surer hands . . .

And after that outstretched so eagerly and confidently for engagement rings, and wedding rings, and jobs . . .

And then, completed, they take up the new, the just beginning, with wonder and pride. Lifting her own child, the new mother marvels, "Isn't he beautiful?" Just look at those tiny hands!

PINK OR BLUE?

YOU WONDER sometimes which is the more lively, the more spirited, the more trouble—little boys or little girls.

Little boys throw things when they get wound up (which is

practically always). They are likely to snatch anything from a cap to a ball to a lamp. Or they take swipes at each other, grab each other with joyous abandon, kick, shriek, hurl each other to the ground, and wrestle like noisy, nipping cubs.

They are a threat to everything on the place, including and especially your nerves. Exposed to them for any length of time, you are likely to think in sheer desperation, "Boys are absolutely and utterly impossible. Give—oh, give me little girls!"

Then the little girls come flocking in. Little girls with their squeals, their screams, their giggles. Little girls are less likely to throw things, but they have other methods of wrecking havoc—such as chasing each other wildly around a table. Or hauling out all your pans, spoons, cups, and glasses for a tea party. Or getting into your lipstick, perfume, hats, evening dresses, and high-heeled shoes. Or dumping boxes of "little people" complete with furniture, dead center of the rug. Most of this to the accompaniment of knife-shrill voices calling bossily to each other, plus such side effects as face-making, tickling, hip and shoulder wiggling, and stuck-out tongues.

Let a herd of little girls take over the premises, and rare is the person who doesn't recall his former plea to heaven and implore, "Give, oh give me little boys!"

PARENTAL PUZZLES

HAVE YOU ever wondered why:

. . . Though you know exactly what your child looks like and don't find his looks any particular treat at home, it becomes of such vital consequence to spot that beaming being as he marches in with the others for a program at church or school. Or why, once located, he is just about the *only* one your eyes can feast upon?

. . . They always get sick on schooldays, rather than bright, sunny weekends?

. . . When they're little they laugh hilariously at your jokes and beg for more? When they're older they say, "Oh, Mother, don't be corny."

. . . Children are so much more eager to help with the work at somebody else's house than at home?

. . . They always seem to look and act their worst when you're most anxious to show them off?

. . . It's so much easier to see how other people should manage their offspring than to know what to do about your own?

. . . They look so unutterably innocent when they're asleep?

PLAYING JACKS

OH, WHAT is so lovely as a circlet of little girls playing jacks? Their bright skirts bloom upon the concrete step. Their knees are bare and brown and their sneakers dirty. Their voices rise and fall like the bouncing ball; they giggle with the same merry tinkle as the raining jacks.

Onesies, twosies. Upsies, downsies, babies in the cradle . . . Sweep the floor . . . Pigs in the pen . . . Go to church.

They exclaim and discuss and argue and laugh.

They get as excited about the old combinations as you once did, and introduce more you've never heard of: Fast Chicago . . . Jack-be-nimble . . . Snake in the grass . . . Fly to the moon . . .

And you remember the thrill of new jacks in your pocket, jingling as you scurried to school. The bright coppery glint of those double-x's. The rubber ball, red as an apple; or the nicked but aristocratic golf balls that briskly spanked the stone and shot to haughty heights.

Little crowds, cohesive as a bridge club, dashed to claim the choicest slabs at school. The undisputed champion was a quiet, angular girl, whose skeletal fingers plucked and scooped with a lovely, awesome, exasperating skill. Though you practiced fervently for hours, you couldn't approach that rare, odd, singular grace that conquered all.

Jacks were easily lost. Reduced to two or three, your store was augmented with rough pebbles found along the lakeshore. Humble, yet charmingly, they glinted when tossed onto the sidewalk.

Now again you hear the leaping ball, the laughter and the arguments, the rainy spatter of the tiny objects flung and deftly snatched. You hear the children reaching out in this time of life's early morning, as children before them reached out in ancient civilizations, playing their games of skill.

The voices, the music of the jacks—a timeless song of history itself.

LITTLE BOYS

Your LITTLE BOY awakes and cries because of a bad dream.

His hot small body clings to you as you sit on the edge of the bed. You feel the firm curves of it through the thin crumpled pajamas. His fat cheeks are moist and the tips of his lashes are moist and fragile, too, against your cheek.

You hold him on your lap and comfort him and know the joy of holding and comforting him, of being his mother to whom he turns when unhappy or afraid.

You think of some fracas in the yard, his demanding in a plaintive howl, "Mummy, help! Billy took my shubble!" And though he is sent back usually to settle the trouble himself, it comes to you with some thrilling sense of wonder and privilege how good it is to be, for this little while, supreme commander of his day. The person omnipotent, who is empowered and entrusted to heal all hurts, answer all questions, meet all his many demands.

And holding and comforting him there in the dark, you think how soon he will be a big leggy boy, remote and roughly shy, not wanting your caresses any more.

And how he will become a man and go away from home and

perhaps do splendid things, things of which you'll boast, but in which life gives no mother any real part. How you will become a shadowy figure to him, someone of whom he thinks with fondness and tenderness and concern, perhaps, but no longer vital or essential to him, because that is life's way.

And it comes to you how brief and filled with glory are these early years of parenthood.

How those who are young mothers are creatures of special privilege, for all the trouble and bother and often unutterable weariness we know. How we should live every moment with our youngsters to the utmost, creating bright memories and hoarding them like riches against the inevitable loss to come.

Few, so tragically few of us, have the faintest conception of what other, older women feel.

"This is my son!" they proudly say, taking a photograph from the mantel and speaking of his accomplishments, while we murmur polite admiration.

This night, however, holding your own little fellow, you begin to understand:

He is lost to them. Gone. But in showing his picture to others, speaking of him to people who can't possibly care, they are recreating him for themselves. Bringing back the little boy who woke up crying in the night, who could be comforted, caressed, and held close against his too swift growing up.

THE FAMILY HEARING AID

A HOUSEWIFE has been described as a combination cook, nurse, laundress, and cleaning woman.

The housewife who is also a mother is all these things and more—she serves as a personnel manager. And not the least of her arts in this respect is that of family listener.

Mothers, I am convinced, develop a phenomenal sense of hearing. Perhaps to compensate for the almost total deafness enjoyed by nearly everyone else in the family.

Sitting exactly three feet across the table from each other, children can hardly convey the simplest messages without, "Huh? What'd you say? Whad'you want? Don't talk with your mouth full. Honestly, Mom, you ought to do something about her manners."

"What she means is she wants to borrow your bike, hers has a flat tire and they're going on this bike hike tomorrow," the mother explains, knowing full well that he can't hear because he doesn't *want* to lend his bike and is trying to divert the whole conversation into a hassle over why his sister talks with her mouth full. Multiply this situation by as many offspring as are gathered at the groaning board, and you will find the typical mother as active as any United Nations interpreter.

Her role is not simplified by the fact that fathers often consume their food groping through such clouds of business concerns that they are only vaguely aware of how many people are present—let alone able to hear clearly the remarks directed their way.

"Who? What coach? What'd he want?" the male parent swims briefly to the surface of discussion. "What's all this about, anyway?"

"Jimmy's coach, dear," his wife tactfully tries to elucidate. "Jimmy was just telling you—there's this new rule about going out for track, and Jimmy feels—"

There must be good reasons why mothers find themselves continually passing the conversational ball, running interference. Standing dead center of the family playing field, we not only are usually tackled first on any issue, we develop a kind of sixth sense about it. An intuitive understanding of who really does mean *what*—and a fervent desire that everybody else get the straight of it, too.

But it's wearing, being the ears of a family. If my own audio powers should ever wane, there will be a hard time selling me a hearing aid!

A CHILD'S BIRTHDAY

WHY are birthdays so enchanting to a child? Beside this signal event every other holiday pales.

"When's my birthday?" they begin to ask, almost as soon as they learn to speak. "How long till my birthday?" And they climb on chairs to consult the calendar, argue mightily as to whose birthday comes first in a family and whose is next and who, therefore, has longest to wait.

Although their very *own* birthday is, of course, supreme, they drain every drop of delight from the birthdays of others. Ah, the ecstasy of birthday secrets—shopping, presents hidden, cards laboriously lettered. And the fun of the mailman's coming:

"You got a present! Here, I'll help you open it." And the ensuing struggle—"Honey, no, it's her birthday, remember, let her—"

And the wistful watching as small clumsy fingers grapple with paper and ribbon. "Oh, boy, gee, look!"

And the fun of helping to bake the cake, of trimming it, lighting the candles with quick scared darts of a match. And the final triumphant procession as the winner of the argument grandly carries it in. The shrill little voices singing, "Happy birthday to yoooo. Happy birthday toooo yooooew!" In these ways they reap vicarious pleasure, and preview their own coming reign . . .

For the youngster having the birthday is indeed king or queen. Special, from the moment of waking. His eyes sparkle. He walks in a proud new way. He must be spanked, of course. And measured—heels flat against the wall and a book upon his head. "How much bigger am I than last year?" he eagerly demands. "How much have I grown?"

And he must ask, no matter how often you've told him, "What time was I born?" And his face wears a special wonder as you explain. He ponders the remarkable fact of his being. How exciting. How marvelous just to have been born!

Is that perhaps why birthdays hold such magic for a child? Perhaps far more than the fact of his presents, he thrills to the gift of—himself.

"We are the guests of existence," Pasternak said . . . And a child is so new a guest.

Oh, to retain that early fervor for living. That first rosy blush of being in love with life itself. To find in each birthday a renewal of wonder at our own creation.

THE BLANKET ROLL

"To make a bedroll, put your oldest and dirtiest blanket on the bottom," your Bluebird directs as you kneel on the living room rug.

"Well, our oldest blankets are at the cabin, but this is certainly the dirtiest one. In fact I ought to wash it—"

"Oh, no, this is lovely, it's real nice and dirty," your daughter enthusiastically approves. "Now you're supposed to put the other things on top and fold the ends."

You gasp as she hands you the instructions. "Why, dear, this doesn't say dirtiest blanket, it only says darkest one."

"Well, dirty means dark, doesn't it? Now come on, let's fold in my boots and stuff."

Mother and daughter take ends of the bulky mess and begin. But objects skid around, and your child giggles. "It sure is lumpy."

"It certainly is. Let's unroll it and start over."

"Daddy ought to be here, he'd fix it."

"Well, women can do these things too—it says here. C'mon, roll."

After three attempts, each sloppier than the last, you give up and settle for what you have. "We seem to be getting worse. Let's tie it. Oh, for Pete's sake, a bowline knot—and I never was a good Girl Scout!"

"This is Campfire Girls."

"Well, the knots, I dread to think, are all the same."

"Just follow the directions."

"Directions are something I've never had much faith in, but let's see. 'A. Lay free end over standing part.' Now this must be the free end—" You get a firm grip on the end of a ball of twine. "But I can't see anything standing, can you?"

"Maybe the boots are standing up inside."

"That's not exactly what they mean. 'B. Bring it through this loop from underneath.'" You can't seem to see any loop either, and the illustrations don't help. "Nuts, let's just forget about the bowline till they teach you, and do it up the best we can."

"Sure, anybody that can tie a package can tie up a blanket, Mom."

It's not that simple, however. Suddenly you seem to have two free ends, and the twine has acquired a squirming life of its own. The ball collapses into a mass of loops and coils that gets worse the harder you strive to encircle and bind the long woolly worm of a so-called blanket roll.

"Don't worry, Mother. Here, I'll help you. Oh, golly, I've got it snarled around my feet."

"Watch out, honey, you're making it worse. Oh, dear, they're out there now, they're honking—and the roll's coming apart!"

You grab a sagging end, stuff objects madly back in, and make a quickly strangling pass with the twine. "Here, give me the scissors, I'll just tie it wherever it sags and cut it off."

"Sure, Mother, don't you worry." She kisses you and struggles the massive monster into her arms. "Just so it holds together till we get to camp. Why, this is okay, this is fine!"

Staggering a little under its bulk, but beaming reassuringly over her shoulder, your Bluebird lugs her blanket roll to the car. As yet, nothing comes spilling out—no toothpaste, soap, nor beans nor candy bar. With fingers crossed, and praying, you return her trusting wave good-by.

HOLD FAST

WATCH IT WITH WONDER, hold it fast—the gangling length of a little boy, the slender, tender dimensions of a fast-growing little girl . . .

You test this state of growing more often than not just after a meal. For you are sitting at the table, and they are just leaving their chairs. It seems you must reach out to them an instant before they go. "Come sit on my lap a minute, let's see how big you are."

And quickly, if sometimes a bit shyly, they oblige. Grinning, they settle themselves upon your inadequate knees. Cocking their heads to show they are really a bit beyond all this, yet with the relaxed enjoyment of animals still taking comfort in the nest, they cuddle, arms about your neck.

"Can't do this much longer, Mother, soon we'll be bigger than you."

"Okay, it'll be my turn then, you'll have to hold me."

They not only fervently promise, the prospect so intrigues them they sometimes insist on clambering down and trying you on their spindly laps for size . . .

To draw near to one another, that is the main thing. To hold each other fast. Physical demonstrations of affection are as needful in the human family as food. To restrain them may be to walk the cold and proper road to adult dignity, but it is also to stunt the emotions and starve the heart.

Hold your children in your arms as long as you can. And when you can't, let them hold you!

TO PUSH A BABY CARRIAGE

A MOTHER tucking her child into a baby carriage is a special and privileged being.

For a carriage arches over something wonderfully new and small and yours alone. Reaching into its cozy confines to check the baby, you too are shielded there, cupped in a safe small shelter that must hark back to the distant days when you were the sleeping infant being made comfortable to his journey into the world of out of doors.

The smell of leather mingles with the scent of fluffy blankets and the sweet scent of a baby just bathed. You arrange the tiny bonneted head on the embroidered pillow, smooth the pretty gift spread. Then down the steps carefully, tilting back, trying not to jolt your precious cargo.

Just to push a baby carriage is a gently satisfying thing. And this too harks back to days distant and half forgotten. The thrill of trundling your very own doll carriage down the street. How maternal little girls feel then; what a sense of power and privilege, to grasp a handle and guide this heavy, protective, joyous, signal vehicle.

There is never a second's loneliness, pushing a baby carriage. Children come rushing up to tag along beside you. Passing people smile and steal a glance. Or parking it a moment before a grocery store, you come out to find someone peeping in. For who can resist the marvel—a human being still so small that he lies sleeping on his tummy in public?

Even walking alone, without contact with other people, there is this secret, quiet, enthralled communion with the passenger so royally propelled.

You smile too, you lean forward to make your presence known. You pause to turn him over, settle him afresh. "See the trees!" you long to say to him, and sometimes do. "See the sky? This is the world, a great big wonderful place that belongs to you too."

The days of pushing a baby carriage do not last long. Some mothers miss it altogether, what with so many errands done by car, and the speed with which strollers appear on the scene. Which seems a pity. Because it's one of the oldest traditions of motherhood, symbolized by a first doll buggy. Just one of those special, brief but beautiful times in a woman's life when she feels complete.

"WHEN I WAS SICK AND LAY ABED"

I WONDER if Stevenson had mothers in mind when he wrote the lines: "When I was sick and lay abed I had two pillows at my head. And all my toys beside me lay to keep me happy all the day."

For who provides the fat white pillows and is called to rearrange them a dozen times a day? As for all the "toys that beside me lay!"

Now according to the picture books Stevenson's ailing patient was quite tidily consoled by a ball, a boat, a bear, and a flock of wooden soldiers. Today's sick-abed son adds to this basic equipment an Erector Set, Tinker Toys, a wood-burning outfit, model airplanes to be assembled, and sometimes a cardboard cupboard filled with dire chemicals.

And no matter *how* sick he is, he not only summons the strength to work with them, but to keep his nurse on a constant trot for such supplies as scissors, paints, pans of water, candles, cardboard boxes, the hammer, the pliers, and the glue.

If the victim (other than you) is a girl, you assemble an entire family of dolls, often with complete wardrobes. And if you've had any experience on the sickroom detail at all, you march right on to your sewing corner to dig out needles, thread, the inevitable scissors, and a bag of bright scraps with which to make additions to the aforementioned wardrobes.

Also you brace yourself for the indubitable call for paper dolls, paint boxes, books, bead stringing sets and sets for the weaving of pot holders, plus such miscellany as pencils, paste, and crayons.

Usually the bed is so full by the time the doctor arrives he can hardly find the patient. You have to make wild scooping motions in order for him to have a place to sit down, let alone write a prescription or hold the medicines.

Ironically enough, by the time evening comes it's the child who feels frisky. In fact, he's usually so revived by his day of rest and attention, he tears out of bed so full of vigor it's all you can do to drive him *back* to bed when it's time to be there.

By then you're so tired you're practically praying for somebody to prescribe a couple of days' complete rest for you.

No wonder a mother secretly groans when a child complains of a morning, "I dooon't feeel goood." Conscientious though our concern, as we anticipate the day's trotting, we dooon't feeel goood either!

SO YOUNG, SO BUSY

How BUSY children are.

"Mother, where's some paper? I simply must have some heavy paper for my dollhouse."

And she burrows through toy cupboards and drawers, hunts down the scissors, the paste. And you see her and her companions on their knees vigorously laboring away.

Or they get out their coloring books and work as fervently as if they were preparing for a show at the gallery. Or they tackle their stick-em books or their embroidery cards. Or, with many pleas for help ("Thread this needle, will you?" "Tie the knot—" "I can't cut it out very well—") make doll clothes.

Or little boys will sweat and pant and heave for hours fashioning a tree house, a fort, a play car out of an old box with roller skates for wheels.

Or they will bang and saw earnestly away, creating a fleet of toy boats, wooden airplanes, or nameless "scientific" gadgets made out of a piece of board, scrap tin, nails, and spools.

However our society may have spoiled them with plastic toys and model kits that stifle half the creative effort, they still manage to fill their hours (and clutter the house) with the things they are continually making, drawing, contriving. Nature has endowed her human young with sheer creative energy which must be expended, whatever the society in which they live.

It is a constant struggle to know what to do with these efforts as you strive to keep order in a house. Throw them all out, the result of so much loving labor? It seems too cruel, somehow. Also, there is the ever-present prospect that some treasure will be missed and demanded the minute it's gone. A mother must be constantly facing such decisions. How much longer will Johnny cling to that insane clutter of lances, sabers, and shields he and a pal have fashioned? After all, they don't play with them any more.

But you know, as you pause in your closet cleaning (and can't help marveling at the ingenuity of the arsenal) that the actual use they have been put to is not the test. They have already served their major purpose, the ships and swords and pictures and paper dolls. And though you cannot resist tucking a few away to be saved, yourself, from sheer sentiment, the majority must be cast out.

However painful it is to be the one who must destroy, you know that something far more vital is constantly being preserved: The experience, the practice, the small but many steps taken forward in the long march of learning.

After all, you think, regarding the house that must be constantly cleaned, the laundry, the dishes, the cooking to be done over and over—woman's work is an endless procession, with each day's result consumed. And the same is true of man.

Perhaps, as children dedicate themselves so avidly to their self-imposed creations, they are only preparing for the routine of life's labors. And discovering, en route, that the reward is in the doing.

A CHILD'S GARDEN

EVERY CHILD should have a little garden all his own.

Let it be close enough to the big folks' garden so that he will feel secure, squatting on his haunches there, becoming intimate with clods and angleworms. But let it be far enough that he may learn the utter loveliness of grubbing the ground alone.

Let it be his kingdom, where he is absolute swaggering potentate. And let it be his farm where he can plant and tend his crops, and reap a bountiful harvest—of radishes, and weeds, and lettuce and carrots and snails, and little jingling rocks, and dreams.

Let his equipment for this patch be his own bright rake, and a red-handled shovel, and a hoe, a trowel, a watering can. And a mother's love. And a dad's sage advice.

Let him have, of course, many gaily colored packets of seeds, to rattle and show to his friends—and open, and spill, and strew in his wobbly rows. And let these seeds be good lively seeds, eager to reach their roots into the soil, quick in their climb toward the sun.

But first let the child know the sweet agony of waiting. Of anticipation. Of a daily rush to look for the miracle. And then just before he loses heart, let the fragile green stripes reward him. Let him drop on all fours to touch the tiny, newborn spears with his fingers. Let his eyes shine. Let him cry out in high, proud excitement, "My garden's up! It grew!"

Let the earth in every child's garden be rich and good, to nurture the things he has planted, and nurture as well his life. . . . Let it smell loamy and lush after a watering, or rain. Let it have a dry baking tingle for his nostrils in the heat of noon. And oh, let him sniff with delight at these earth scents, breathe them deep into his being. Let him sense in some buried core of his own

Reprinted from *Better Homes and Gardens* magazine.

awareness that it is earth's fertility and finality that makes him kin to God.

Let the child get dirt on his hands and streaked across his face. Let him sweat as he hacks with his hoe and pulls at those thrillingly wild and stubborn enemies, the weeds. Let him learn what it is to be tired and hot and dirty with labor and never to be ashamed.

And let the beetle bugs come, and the foraging rabbits, and all the countless creatures, winged or footed or crawling, that with such innocent, driving purpose take unto themselves a portion of what men grow. Let a child discover their ways, along with the ways of seeds and sun. . . . Let him lie for a dreamy spaceless time upon his tummy, watching the progress of a furry caterpillar. And hearing the soft, bullet thudding of grasshoppers; the swift scurrying of bunnies and chipmunks—and maybe a thieving elf, or a sprite or two. For overhead, let the sky be so blue, the clouds so whitely gliding, all things in children's gardens take on a magical quality.

Let the child reap the results of his efforts. A fistful of saucy-tailed radishes. Some spindly carrots, too thickly planted, of course, and not thinned. A saucepan of peas, half-spilled before reaching the house. Long, lumpy green pendants of beans. . . . Let at least one meal be glorified by a mother's boast, "Joey raised nearly everything on the table." And let the child know that most splendid fulfillment of all—producing enough of something to give away.

Let every growing child have a garden all his own!

A TENT

CHILDREN must all be the descendants of nomads, for they would live their lives out, if you let them, in a tent.

They discover the joy of this triangular shelter when they are very young. Let any mother start airing blankets on a line, and her offspring are sure to come scurrying between the blankets' flapping sides.

"A tent! A tent!" they shout in delight. "This will be my tent and that pink one yours. We'll be neighbors and live in our tents."

Sometimes they prevail on their mother to string up a line especially for the purpose and over it drape an old unused spread or quilt. Staked to the ground with little sticks, it makes a lovely tent. There, with their dolls and their dishes and their little toy stoves, they set up housekeeping, crawling joyfully in and out to obtain crackers and jelly sandwiches and to pick tiny bouquets of clover or dandelions. They urge you to creep in on all fours— into this cozy, sun-fragrant, grassy haven, where they crouch in such delight.

When they are older, they must have a real canvas tent to make their pleasure complete. A waterproof tent, where they can be snug even in a shower. A place where they can sometimes "sleep out." A tent to take on camping trips. Every summer, their dad digs it out from under the porch and aids in setting it up in the yard.

And there, for a few days, it becomes the social center of the neighborhood. Club meetings are held there, and tea parties, and fights. And the inevitable pleas bombard you: "Oh, please, may we sleep out tonight? Let us sleep in the tent!"

This, too, usually brings on arguments. The little ones want to join the big ones and their friends, which is unthinkable: "We want to *talk!* Besides there isn't room." The boys want it the same night as the girls. "And don't forget whose tent it really is," some long-forgotten claim is laid. "I got it for Scouts, remember. So it's *my tent!*"

And when some of these matters are settled, the most elaborate plans go oft awry. Mosquitoes, a hoot owl, an unexpected fright ("We heard this *terrible noise!*") will send a covey of girls tearing to the house, clutching their sheets. And even when they do finally settle down and get to sleep, *you* can't. They're so crowded, how do they stand it? And it's chilly. Have they got enough blankets? You toss and turn and worry and finally steal outside with a flashlight. Cautiously, you lift the flap and peer in.

And there, crammed together on the hard ground, they are blissfully snoozing. Close to nature, close to their primordial ancestors, no doubt, they are sleeping the sleep of the wild, the free, the innocent; the peaceful sleep of the young, when all the world is new and summertime is eternal—in a tent.

"PLEASE MAY WE GO SWIMMING?"

THOSE WHO CLAIM that all life began in the ocean must surely have children.

Even infants have an affinity for water that must spring from deep wells of the past.

The baby, still too wobbly to hold up his head, loves to be lowered into his bath. And it becomes the major event of his day when he is old enough to be able to play and splash.

Then when the wonderful world of water is discovered outside the home his ecstasy is boundless—and adamant. Observe the small fry in any wading pool. Except for the occasional youngster who is terrified, the only screams you hear are those of pleasure —or of angry protest at being hauled out.

As they grow older their love for water seems to become more desperate, a need. "Oh, please may we go swimming? Please, please, please!" And heaven help the parent who for reasons of his own must deny that frenzied imploring, for it is like bucking some natural force that is as strong as the ocean itself.

Almost no child will ever leave water of his own volition. He must be called, exhorted, threatened, and sometimes dragged bodily from its liquid embrace. And rare indeed is the time when he is too cold, or too sunburned, or too waterlogged to stay out if there is the slightest chance to go swimming again. In fact, barely is he dried, fed, and diverted toward some other course of action before he is beginning to whine, then to argue, then to plead.

My own would go swimming five or six times a day, if allowed. In fact, they seem to draw some peculiar sustenance from the water, some nourishment that makes mere meals unnecessary.

Sometimes when they are swimming I have the eerie feeling that they must be watched lest in some moment when I'm not looking they sprout fins and disappear.

And whenever I hear myself saying things like, "No, you can't go swimming, it's too cold—" Or, "Now you come right in this minute or you can't go tomorrow—" echoes of my own parents' voices rise in my ears. I remember so acutely it is like pain, standing on a dock that rocked beneath my feet, and gazing down, down into the gray-blue wonder of it all. And knowing that if I were not allowed to plunge into it at once, to merge with it, explore it, identify with it completely with body and spirit, my soul would die.

A child's need and love for water is instinctive and eternal.

LITTLE GIRLS TOGETHER

How DELIGHTFUL is the friendship that exists between little girls. Small females somewhere between the ages of six and ten.

When they are smaller they will quarrel over toys. They cry and get mad and go home. When they are older they compete. They will hurt each other's feelings. Many times they talk mercilessly about each other, even the closest chums. They can weep their hearts out on a pillow over a real or fancied snub.

But when they are first grade playmates, or second, or third or fourth, then they are still exactly that: Companions in play. In secrets. In giggling games. In merry undertakings which include everything from baking a package cake to selling cold drinks, or organizing a back yard show or a Witch's Club.

Their laughter is as sparkling and without malice as a bright morning shower. Their jokes are bold, obvious, usually old as the stars, and utterly without guile. They make up insane songs with which to accompany their rope jumpings, or the bouncing of a ball. They call each other up mornings and evenings to giggle, exchange lengthy lists of what they hope to get for their birthdays, and make vast impossible plans for building a playhouse or buying a horse.

Spending the night together is a thrilling undertaking which involves lugging along a bulging bag of stuffed animals as well as their best pajamas, robe, slippers, bubble bath, and at least one doll with complete wardrobe. They climb joyously from bed to bed, bounce, throw pillows, and keep each other awake with scary stories.

At last, after many remonstrances and warnings, they collapse into the profound sleep of childhood. Stealing in, you find them sprawled in incredible positions, legs dangling over the bedside, pigtails or curls awry, covers trailing the floor. They are usually awake at dawn, singing, cavorting, and buzzing like bees over their marvelous plans for the day.

Little girls playing together in this wonderful morning of their lifetime are like young birds chirping, or butterflies winging lightly among the flowers. They need each other in a way that is instinctive and joyous; they are nourished by each other's presence, they thrive and grow strong in the light of each other's warmth, as plants grow unconsciously upward in the light of the sun.

THEY'RE ONLY LITTLE ONCE

Two SMALL NAKED BOYS splash wildly in the big white tub, their bodies shiny under the bathroom lights. The older flails the water and hurls it into his little brother's excited, uplifted rosy face. He doesn't mind. Blinking, rubbing his face and eyes, he shrieks with delight and tries vainly to hurl the water back.

They thresh about, grabbing for the soap; they throw their

sodden washcloths. Their hair plasters their heads like the feathers of drowned birds.

Patiently and helplessly you sit waiting with the towels, urging them to stop, to get out, with a kind of rhythmic hopelessness. Finally you pull the plug, though they still flail about like seals, sliding down the tub's edge, trying to chin themselves on the towel bars. The younger laughs, makes faces, imitates his big brother's every antic.

Finally, meaning business, you haul one out bodily, and the other hastily scrambles. The older seems suddenly long-legged, rangy and limby beside the younger's chubby curves as—with much cavorting, he sketchily dries himself. You grab more towels and give both a vigorous rubbing, from the head down. You don't risk letting them hold the talcum powder, not tonight! Lifting high the can you give them each a brief dousing and shoo them out.

"They're only little once," you remind yourself for the tenth time, mopping up.

Thank goodness!

PACKED SUITCASES

LIFE is a long long journey, marked by a line of luggage through which you can almost trace a woman's biography:

There are her first childish belongings put excitedly into a satchel for that first visit to Grandma, or to spend the night with a friend.

And after that the slightly larger bag that she fills with such eager anticipation for a sojourn to camp.

And then the trunks to be arranged and rearranged, with a mother's hovering help, then carried on a father's stout shoulders, as she prepares for college.

And the shining dignity and wonder of cases that she fills with all the secret lovely things for her wedding journey.

And the small bag packed, often weeks ahead, patiently awaiting the joyous dash to the hospital to have her first baby . . .

Somehow all this comes flooding poignantly back as we supervise the packing of our own children's bags:

A small boy eagerly stuffing his new, very own suitcase with his toothbrush, his favorite pajamas, and a rabbit dirty and worn from loving, getting ready to go to the hospital to have his tonsils out.

The earnest inventory of socks and sheets and swimming suits as a son or daughter also pack up for camp.

The hauling down of dusty trunks from the attic to see if they'll hold the countless things that our offspring must carry away to college.

The suitcases lying open upon a bed, being filled by another starry-eyed girl before another wedding trip.

The catch in the throat as you come across it later, standing patiently waiting in another hallway—the small bag filled with the tiny garments for your grandchild's first homecoming . . .

Life is all too swift a journey!

A CHILD'S HAND IN YOURS

WHAT FEELING in all the world is so nice as that of a child's hand in yours?

It is soft. It is small and warm. It is as innocent and guileless as a rabbit or a puppy or a kitten huddling in the shelter of your clasp. Or it is like living clay to be molded. It is the essence of all trust.

"Here I am," it seems to tell you. "Shape me. Guide me. Lead me."

If you stop to consider, the responsibility it imposes is almost too much. But you don't. "Here, take my hand while we're crossing the street," you say, and concentrate on the immediate business of getting him safely to the curb. Or, "Hold onto my hand,

Mother will see that the dog doesn't bite you, don't be afraid."

Or you take the feverish, betrayed little fingers in yours after the tonsils are out and say, "I know it hurts, darling, but it won't last long. Just hang onto my hand until you fall asleep."

A child's hand in yours—what tenderness it arouses, what almost formidable power it conjures up! You are instantly not only the symbol but the very touchstone of security, wisdom, and strength.

Though you may secretly know yourself to be lacking in all these things, miraculously the child endows you with them as he reaches up. As he clutches your own hand so unquestioningly, he is giving back the very qualities that he draws from that hand to comfort himself.

He is making you taller and stronger and wiser. He is leading you just a little nearer to the person he imagines you to be.

And a child's hand in yours is something more. It is your link with life itself. For each son or daughter is a projection of those who created him.

A mother clasping her little girl's hand, a father gripping the fingers of his small son—each is leading his own dreams forward, holding fast to his own tomorrows.

The Man You Married

There is nothing stronger and nobler than when man
and wife are of one heart and mind in a house, a grief
to their foes, and to their friends great joy, but their
own hearts know it best.

—Homer

IN DEFENSE OF AMERICAN MEN

DON'T TELL ME the average American male is becoming soft. There have been a spate of articles decrying this so-called "trend," and personally I resent every one of them.

Recently I climbed down off the roof where I was helping my husband build a house, to relax and read. Here I'd had a lot of fun swinging a hammer and even mixing cement, all the while visualizing myself as a sturdy pioneer woman helping her mate wrest a home from the wilderness. According to this article before me I'd been all wrong: Men should be men, and women women —and never should their traditional duties overlap. Above all, and particularly, men should be above such menial pursuits as helping with the housework or putting a bevy of kids to bed.

Then there are the patently false stereotypes of Dad foisted on us by stories and cartoons that depict him as a kind of ineffectual nincompoop. But these seem to me no more false than the stereotypes of the stern Victorian father who never deigned to dry a dish, and ruled the roost. If we were transported to the Good Old Days I suspect that we'd find far fewer of these archetypes than is popularly supposed.

My own father's boast was that he'd washed dishes for my mother the night they met and been doing it every night for forty years. I also cherish happy memories of his bathing his little flock, then with one on each arm of his squeaky rocker and one on his lap, singing us all to sleep.

My mother was not a dominating woman, and she practiced no career. My father worked long and hard at very masculine labor. He did these things for the selfsame reason that thousands of good men do them still: Because he loved his wife and children. And these tasks were the most enjoyable way he knew of to express that love.

American men are not sissies. They're simply wonderful husbands!

HOW TO MAKE A HUSBAND HAPPY

IT'S THE LITTLE THINGS that speak subtly yet most reassuringly of love in a home. When it comes to husbands, we so often take them for granted.

We are so busy mothering the children we forget that men are secretly but grown-up little boys inside, and they'd sometimes like a bit of inconspicuous mothering and looking after, too.

Here are some of the little things a woman can do for hers:

Make sure his shirts are done the way he likes them, whether by yourself, the maid, or the laundry. And if the laundry, that they're taken and delivered on time. Also that the buttons are on . . .

Press and have clean and available his favorite ties . . .

Occasionally (though don't make a habit of it) shine his shoes . . .

Take care of his clothes. See that his suits are safely gotten to and from the cleaner's and in good repair . . .

Refrain from attempting to take care of his stamp or coin collections, his fishing or hunting gear, or his tools . . .

Buy food and cook it with his preferences in mind. Surprise him sometimes with a special dish . . .

Make just as much fuss over his birthday as you like him to make over yours. And on your wedding anniversary, buy him a card . . .

Keep the day's mail in a convenient place where he can find and enjoy it when he gets home . . .

Don't let the children dissect the evening paper before he can get to it . . .

Train them not to bombard him with pleas and problems the

minute he walks in, and don't do so yourself. Wait until after dinner when he's relaxed and more in a mood to cope.

FATHERS AND MOTHERS—
DIFFERENT GOALS

WHAT MOST PARENTS want above all else for their children is happiness and success.

And while generalizations never fit all cases, it seems to me that mothers are more often striving for the happiness, the fathers for the success.

Women are with their children so much that we become keenly attuned to their moods and emotions, their secret (and often not so secret) desires. Women are like sensitive instruments that not only continually pick up and record their offspring's heartbeats, but react in kind.

When they hurt, we hurt. When they rejoice our own spirits soar. When they need or desperately want something, we often want it for them even more.

Women, in the interest of their children, are continually anticipating, laying plans. It is the mothers, usually, who arrange for dancing or music lessons, preview a neighborhood to gauge its social suitability for their young, arrange to get tickets for children's concerts, interview teachers, do what they can for good schools.

And men have a great and genuine share in all this. It is the men who cheerfully pay the bills, haul the progeny to their mother-maneuvered destinations, physically participate. Because men, bless them, want the good life too, for their sons and daughters. But in a subtly different way. Men want to be proud of their children; they want them to succeed.

It seems to me that a woman's approach is primarily emotional. While children's "happiness" is of less immediate concern to men than the knowledge that they are soundly prepared to meet and triumph over life's vicissitudes.

A DAD, A BOY, AND A CAR

IT BEGINS when they're about fourteen, this curious disease of wanting to drive, work on, own a car.

There is no inoculation against it, and no medicine as yet discovered that will ease its pangs—either for the victim or his father. Nor are there any vitamins that will fortify these two males for the long struggle ahead. But patience will go a long way. And love. And on the father's part, a large dose of remembering how he suffered when this particular malady struck him.

Some of its early symptoms are the pleas: "Let me steer." "Hey, I'll back it out of the garage." Or long puzzling periods when the boy will merely sit in the car, fumbling with its controls.

A slightly later manifestation is the desire to take a car apart. The average car-struck lad will want to peer under hoods, examine parts, try his hand at taking spark plugs out. The desire does *not* always make him want to change a tire or wash the thing, though if he is very far gone he will do so. Constant throughout is the frenzy simply to ride in cars. To go along with guys who have their drivers' permits, or those dashing heroes who own their own cars.

Constant too is the amazing ability to identify the make, model, and characteristics of every vehicle that passes. A boy who can't remember who discovered America, or when, or correctly identify any three parts of speech, will rattle off: "There was this 1958 blue hardtop convertible Mercury coming from the right, and there was this guy in a '64 Mustang trying to pass from the left—" Cars are the topic of conversation from dawn to dark.

The father may as well teach, or have his son taught, to drive as soon as it's legally permissible. If he does this himself his off-spring, he finds, already knows most of what to do—or thinks he does, and the results can be even more harrying than trying to teach his wife. A hired, emotionally uninvolved instructor is heartily advised.

Once the boy is licensed, the most painful phase of the whole affliction sets in. Two burning issues rock the household now: "Can I have the car?" And, "When can I buy a car?"

The first is never really settled, but must be resolved in soul-searching misery time after time. The second involves a merciless bombardment of propositions: "There's this ad in the paper for this '59 Olds—all I need is two thousand dollars—" It means arduous, anguishing discussions of jobs, budgets, payments, up-keep, and insurance.

Once the deed is done, the parent is due for a whole new rash of pains and problems. Dad, who's been comforted to think, "Well, at least it's not a piece of junk," is likely to look out the window and go into mild shock. The beautiful, civilized, just-bought car is being stripped of its chrome, having its rear end lowered, subjected to the indignities of leading, and a paint job of passionate purple. The whole topped off with a Confederate flag and a flying girl-friend scarf.

As if this shuddering spectacle weren't enough, Dad must gird his loins afresh to do battle with hours, homework, and possible traffic tickets. As for the insurance—that alone consumes hours as he copes with the question: How best can he protect the safety of this young driver, and that of the public?

It's a curiously American manifestation, this of the car-happy adolescent. It comes about because of a culture of prosperity, perhaps. And freedom. And of men and boys who used to fight a wilderness, but now fight—traffic. And sometimes each other. Perhaps there is no explanation for it, just as there is no real cure.

But it's sure to strike almost every family. And there's some-thing zesty and wonderful about it, at that. About the whole combination—a dad, a boy, and a car.

DADDY CAN FIX IT

FATHER can fix it. Or Daddy, as little folks call him. Or, as they get older, Pop or Dad.

Whatever his title, there's nothing like that remarkable do-it-yourself but do-it-for-everybody-else male parent.

Often his ingenuity surges to the front even before his offspring arrive, as he fashions a crib, a feeding table. More, today's dad enjoys bathing and feeding his babies sometimes, rocking them, telling them stories. And when they come running in with a broken toy, how many a lucky wife can console, "Don't cry. Wait till Daddy gets home. Your father can fix it."

Daddy can fix it. Anything, everything. Radios, clocks, a bike, a pair of roller skates. A doll, a leaky boat, an eyeless stuffed rabbit. Or those antiques his wife is always dragging home from auction sales. Patiently, cleverly, with glue and tape and nails, and paint and love and imagination—whatever the object, if it's dear to its owner, somehow, some way, he'll devise the means of its salvation.

Father can fix it. Often he will even build it. A playhouse, a picnic table, a fireplace, a wall, a patio in the yard.

Handyman—yes, he's usually that, but more important, he's the family handyman in matters of the heart. Report cards. Budding romances. Times of illness, worry, family strain. That complication in the Cub Scouts, that looming problem at church, at school—don't worry, talk it over with Dad. Dad will analyze the whole thing wisely, come up with the proper solution, make you realize it's not so grave a complication, after all. Or if it proves to be—well, your father will be standing by.

Daddy can fix it. Dad will get it for you. That costume for the play, though it means a trip clear across town. The supplies you need for the bazaar. That last-minute birthday present. Those pretzels and cold drinks for the teen-age party. And regularly, with the car crammed with little folks, groceries at the super-market on Friday night.

Father can fix it. Find it, get it, pay for it, help you figure it out. Here's to him, bless him—the one who lives at our house, and at yours. The American dad!

FATHER'S DAY EVERY DAY

"Your mother's a wonderful cook," my father used to say—some-times in her presence, but just as often not. Or, "Isn't Mama pretty? Really, she's one of the best-looking women in town."

And time after time she would remark of him: "Dad's so good to all of us. We certainly should be thankful to have a father like him."

Neither of them had the faintest idea of influencing their chil-dren by such comments; they were simply statements straight from the heart. Yet subtly, constantly, such words were helping to shape a pleasant and goodly image of the other parent in their children's minds.

All too often in the battle of the sexes offspring are sought as allies. "Just look at that mess," a woman will berate her husband. "Daddy's so careless, he never picks up a thing." Or, taking out her own frustrations and disappointments, "We could have a beautiful home too if your father had a better head for business like Uncle Bob."

Or a woman will use a father as the perpetual expender of punishment and bogeyman. "You'll be sorry, just you wait till your father gets home!"

Men are less prone to attack their wives in this backhanded manner, and when they do it's often disguised as a joke: "Where's your baseball bat? Why, Mom probably threw it out—you know how she is when she gets on a cleaning spree." Or, "I know how you feel when she nags you, boy, look how she picks on me."

All parents have their differences; there are things about each other they'd very much like to change. And there are sometimes occasions when one may treat a youngster in a manner which seems to the other outrageously unfair. Sometimes, in the cause of sheer human justice, the other must take a stand.

Even so, criticizing one's mate to his child is fraught with danger. It not only seems disloyal, it's building within that youngster a feeling of wretched ambivalence. He is divided, pulled this way and that. Instead of loving his parents fully, completely, as a unit, he feels impelled to choose up sides, and often he pits one against another.

Regardless of all this, mothers and dads can do a great deal for the children by forming the habit of sincere appreciation, voiced spontaneously and frequently: "Just listen to Mother, sewing away on that dress for Jane to wear to the party—what a wonderful person she is." . . . Or, "Wasn't it nice of Dad to drive this whole gang to Scout camp? You kids should be very grateful to have a father like that."

THE ART OF COMMUNICATION

COMPLAINTS run rife these days from husbands and wives who seem to have lost the art of communication.

Why, women demand, don't their husbands go to as much effort to make good conversation at home as they do at the office or their clubs? Why don't they ever tell us anything? And why, men echo the outcry, can't women learn the essential technique of really listening to or talking with a man?

For marriage may be said to be a blend of both sound and silence. When a sense of unity and fellowship pervades both phases, the marriage cannot help be firm and good. But when the sound is all one-sided, or the silence of either too prolonged, loneliness and subtle estrangements set in.

Here are some suggestions for both husband and wife to consider in closing the breach:

1. Be understanding. Don't try to wrest conversation from a person who's obviously tired. "Women simply have no idea what a man's up against out in the business world," as one man says. "Often he comes home not only acutely worried but exhausted."

2. Show interest. Give your undivided attention to what the other does tell you, even though the soup be scorching or you're missing a vital play on the televised football game.

3. Be an enthusiastic audience, but don't interrupt to show it.

4. Don't criticize. Be tolerant of the other's speech faults.

5. Find out what your own are and correct them.

6. Never betray a confidence. Keep all intimate discussions about business, the neighbors, or your own personal problems strictly between yourselves.

7. Keep your emotions under control. Lots of times men don't confide in their wives or vice versa because the other is likely to react too strongly to what he or she is being told.

8. Share the other person's interests. Learn everything you possibly can about his or her profession, sport, or hobby.

9. Cultivate new mutual interests that will give you common food for discussion.

10. Try to keep alive a free, unself-conscious expression of vital issues. People who know each other intimately often grow embarrassed about exposing their deepest thoughts. Yet most of us need spiritual companionship even more than we need small talk.

ARE YOU DEBIT OR CREDIT?

"EVERY WIFE is either a credit or a detriment to her husband," says my sister Gwen emphatically, "there are no in-betweens."

As the veteran wife of a school superintendent, she has witnessed a long parade of women who either help or hinder their husbands' careers. There is the bossy wife who tries to dominate the system and the town. There is the meek and mousy wife who never takes part in anything. There is the jealous wife, the home-sick wife, the social-climbing wife . . . Against these there are all the good, wise, personable, and often talented wives of whom the man, his boss, and even the school board can be proud.

Having disposed of educators' wives, we got to talking about wives in general. Particularly the woman who seems to have no special gifts. My sister Gwen insists that such a woman, to be a genuine credit to her husband, should develop talents of her own.

Be a good homemaker, which doesn't mean getting obnoxious about ashtrays and dirty feet. But at least hurl yourself into the joys of keeping a tidy, attractive house, so that if a business associate drops in your husband will be able to entertain him in a neat living room.

Be a good cook. Not necessarily a gourmet, nor a woman who toils her life away under the impression that the way to a man's heart (or success) is through the kitchen, but cook so that his meals are hearty, appetizing, and reasonably on time. Or be a wife whose husband can invite the boss to dinner, or expansively offer to have the staff party at his house, knowing you'll come up with something not only delicious but fairly original.

Be his personal valet. See that his clothes are back from the cleaner's when they should be, with all buttons intact. See that his shirts are flawless, his ties on the ready. That he gets a haircut when he needs one, even if you have to nag or threaten to shear him yourself.

See that his children are presentable most of the time—not only physically as clean as children are sensibly supposed to be, but that their manners do him no discredit. A man's prestige sags almost tangibly when he's embarrassed by a brat. See that it's never said, "I like old Harry and his wife, but take those kids away."

And when you go out with him, be as chic and charming as it's within your power to be. This doesn't mean striving to be a beauty or a fashion plate, but at least that your clothes are not too hopelessly dated, and that you are tidily groomed. (No dandruff on the collar, no tortured stocking seams.)

Also, bone up on what others are likely to be talking about. Be a good conversationalist—but not so good that you outtalk everyone else. Especially your husband.

As for the wife who is talented in other fields, who has outside accomplishments—she has to be twice as good in all the foregoing so her husband and his friends won't think she's neglecting him.

TWO LITTLE SOMEDAY-MEN

EVERY DAY about three the doorbell rings and they come bounding up the steps to pay you a visit—two little second grade boys.

Their mothers don't mind. The one who works acknowledges that she's glad there's somebody to give Randy a hug and maybe a cookie after school. Someone to make a fuss over his papers and drawings. As for the other one, she understands if Tony's a few minutes late. "Thank goodness," she says, "there are a few people left in the world who still like little boys."

Who still like little boys . . .

Boys with their shirttails out and their pant legs trailing. Little boys with their shining eyes and their big ear-to-ear smiles. Little boys who smell of crayons and bubble gum and dirt and grass and out-of-doors.

True, they are sometimes pests, these two-legged beginners in the mysterious and troublesome business of living. They track and spill and fight and break your lamps with their baseballs. They trample your lawns and climb your trees and snitch your apples and play havoc sometimes with your flowers. They write on sidewalks; they throw stones, they yell, they boast, they argue, they tell tall tales, they quarrel.

There are times when you could cheerfully bash their heads together—your own small male offspring and those of the neighbors. Times when you wonder why their Maker didn't simply skip the phase between their strollers and their first automobiles. For their own sake you sometimes wonder. For it must be hard to be a noisy, untidy, scolded, berated, unwelcome little boy.

They seem tough, it's true, these little guys. They don't seem to mind when people order, over and over, "Now you stop that, get out of here, go away!" They beat a hasty retreat, still jaunty, undaunted. But I wince whenever I see or hear it.

Little boys . . . little boys . . . So young, so new, so unsuspecting of what tomorrow has in store.

So soon to be candidates for the awkwardness, the secret agonies of adolescence. Soon, all too soon, to have their hearts broken by girls. And soon, oh much too soon, to be rebels, fighting for their identity in a confused and troubled world.

And soon—so terribly soon to be put into uniform and sent away from home. So far away, some of them, where they'll know loneliness and fear, and even give their lives, some of them, in the conflicts we manage to be involved in, whether or not we're at war.

And after that the cares of marriage will be upon them all too soon. The adult male longings, the sometimes impossible dreams: To be loved and respected by their wives. To have children they can be proud of. To provide well for their families in an age when families demand so much. To succeed.

Sometimes you see not the spindly, pesky, lovable, noisy little fellow—you see in his stead the tall, strong, yet somehow tragically burdened man he will one day be.

And so when the doorbell rings and they call, "It's us!" you call back, "Well, good, come on in. If there's one thing I like to see about this time of day it's two little boys."

"WHAT BECAME OF THE GIRL
I MARRIED?"

LOST: One gay, sweet bride. Girl who thinks I'm wonderful and tells me so. Chief characteristic: Appreciation! Ample reward offered by one discouraged guy.

COUNTLESS HUSBANDS could have composed that ad.

In the main, we women do a good job on our homes, our children, our community undertakings, and making ends meet. We don't come off too badly on the score of personal appearance, and most of us love our mates with depth and loyalty and passion. But far too many of us fall flat on our faces when it comes to showing those mates any real understanding or appreciation.

We fail in the first place, I believe, because we were not realistically prepared for marriage. Most of us floated down the aisle believing that our particular orange blossoms would never fade. Many a wife, instead of accepting her quite human but often quite wonderful husband for what he is, remains stubbornly in love with the prince of the fairy tales. And she will shove, shame, nag, weep, plead, and connive to try to fit her bewildered partner into the princely mold. That she knows it's impossible is beside the point. For she has also fallen in love with another deadly mirage: her own sense of having been wronged.

The woman who has formed the habit of thinking herself neglected is reluctant to relinquish the role even when she can! The very invitation she has been clamoring for, a date to go dancing or out on the town, is rejected: "You know I haven't anything decent to wear." (To come right down to it, she'd rather stay home than give up that precious: "You never take me anywhere.")

More women would find their longings fulfilled if they realized that romance is a two-way street. The wife who sits dourly at one

Reprinted from *Better Homes and Gardens* magazine and *Reader's Digest*.

end of it expecting love to come to her had better be prepared to sit a long time! But she who is willing to hop down from her high horse and come running halfway (and a little more) will find all her marriage relationships enriched.

For men like attention too. There are almost no men who do not feel a responsive leap when they are praised by their wives, told: "You're wonderful; I'm proud of you; I'm glad you're mine."

Before complaining too loudly of neglect, women should ask themselves honestly—who has the best of it? We may bear the children and rear them. We may wash, iron, clean, cook, quick-freeze, sew. But most of us have conveniences to make the going easier. And no law says we have to do these things.

A man, on the other hand, becomes an economic slave the minute he signs the marriage license. He is linked forever not only to the girl of his dreams but to his desk, or whatever means he has for her support. Because support her he must—and likewise any children she bears him. Morally and legally, he alone is responsible, and little short of death itself will ever free him. For even in case of separation or divorce this burden continues.

Just as a woman is under constant advertising pressure to be "alluring," a man gets constant financial pressure. He is attacked in his most vulnerable spot—his wife and kids. Take them vacationing in this roomier car; make them cooler with air conditioning, safer with fencing. And the most potent pleas come from the family itself: "The Beckers have bought a summer place, *why can't we?*"

Small wonder that so many men bury themselves in the financial pages, instead of whispering sweet nothings to their wives.

It may be true that husbands too often take love for granted, but women too often take for granted the responsibilities men assume for them. Ask any widow who is suddenly faced with the need to carry on alone. "When you have a good husband, you just don't realize how much he does," she will tell you. "Not until you're actually in his shoes can you appreciate what he's been up against. Then it's too late."

But for most of us it's not too late. Thank your husband for taking such good care of you—starting now. Praise him to his folks, his friends, and his offspring. Be grateful for his every little kindness—and show it!

If you are one of those who have been in love with your own misery, there is a good way to end the affair: write yourself a letter. Turn a searchlight on your own faults, and list them honestly. Then set down every lovable trait, accomplishment, and quality of the man you married. You'll find such positive action a revelation in values, and you'll rise from it a far more appreciative, hence *lovable* wife.

Understanding and appreciation. The woman who can rediscover those virtues won't have to worry about romance. She'll have her share of it, and something even better—a guy who'll be saying, in his heart: *"Found: the girl I married."*

"DAD, I NEED SOME MONEY"

To ME, one of the most touching gestures a man makes is that old familiar one of reaching into his hip pocket and drawing forth his leather wallet.

"Touching is right!" he'd probably say, laughing, if you mentioned it. For day in and day out, he's being touched for money.

"Dad, this is cracker-money day, and also I've got to have a new notebook." . . . "Dad, I've got a big date tonight. How about getting my allowance early?" . . . "Don't forget to leave me some money, dear. The maid's coming today, and I think I'll take advantage of that shoe sale downtown."

Cheerfully, patiently, automatically, he produces that faithful source of supply. Without complaint, he doles it out—the change for the children, the pay for the cleaning woman, the cash you specify. "Now, you sure that's enough? Here's a little extra, just in case."

Sometimes he's forced to protest. If the bank account is low, he has to say so. But you know that it hurts him to do so, and he'll put it off as long as he can. He'd far rather cut corners and do without himself than deny his family the things they need or would like to have. For he cherishes that age-old American tribute —"a good provider." To be able to take care of his own is a matter of masculine pride.

He also likes to hold up his end of things with other men. How often during the day he reaches for his wallet—to pay a cab fare, pick up the check at lunch, donate to some cause or drive. And then, when he gets home at night, the whole family campaign starts up again: "Honey, the paper boy is at the door." . . . "There's a man collecting for the Salvation Army." . . . "Judy's leaving for her music lesson. She'll have to have three dollars for it."

And watching the hand travel to the familiar spot, you realize: "This is the hand that works for us."

And you remember your father's big brown calloused hand making that selfsame journey, to produce an old-fashioned snap purse, from which he brought forth funds. And you think of all the hands of men throughout the country, going back and forth to the hip pocket, like faithful pendulums, in this timeless cause.

"Dad, I need some money." How many billfolds that plea wears out! No wonder husbands so often need new ones for birthdays or Christmas. The billfolds get tired and worn and thin; eventually, they give up.

But the men? Tired and worn though they too may become, somehow they can't just quit, and they seldom give up. They are made of tougher, finer leather, sewed with sinews much too strong. So long as there's life in their bodies and love in their hearts and somebody to say, "Dad, I need some money," they manage to keep on filling the wallets. And reaching for them.

HE LEADS HIS FAMILY HOME

THE MOTOR begins to sputter one night on the lonely road to your country place. "Oh, no, don't tell me we're out of gas," your husband says. He cuts the motor and coasts downhill, everybody straining forward as if to lend strength. As the car comes to an inexorable stop, he roots through the glove compartment and groans afresh: *"Who took that flashlight?"*

Naturally, nobody can imagine. "Well, you sit here and wait. I'll walk up to the next cabin to see if they can lend us some gas. Or some kind of a light, at least."

He trudges off through the shadows, while you huddle together in a kind of snug alarm. "What if a robber should come along?" the children scare themselves. "What if a bear should come out of the woods? Maybe the dog should've gone along to protect Daddy!"

"Now hush," you tell them nervously. "He'll be right back with some gas—we hope." Guiltily you remember the flashlight back home in the closet where you were using it digging out winter wraps.

A little eternity drags by before a welcome eye comes swinging back down the road. "Well, everybody out, we'll have to walk. They didn't have any gas, but at least they lent us a light to see by."

"You mean *walk?* All the way? It must be a mile!"

"Be thankful it isn't two. C'mon, you kids each grab a cat. And don't let 'em get away," he warns. "If they get lost in these woods they might never find their way home."

The dog bounds ahead, barking lustily. "Good for Belle, she'll scare away the bears," somebody says. "Or the snakes."

"Snakes!"

"Now there's nothing to be afraid of," the head of the household says firmly. "See how bright the stars are. And notice how good the trees smell."

The stars indeed are glittering overhead. The earth has a spicy fragrance. The night things begin to sing a kind of marching tune. And almost before you know it, there is the cabin on its rise of ground, its dark shape a welcome friend as it keeps vigil beside the shining lake.

"Well, here we are," your husband says. "Now all you kids and cats get to bed while I carry some gas back to the car."

Cheerfully he sets off alone, carrying the heavy gas can. And as the small eye of the flashlight disappears over the hill you think of men the wide world over doing the tough, the lonely jobs that keep a family going—and lead it safely home.

The Wonderful World of Women

Their tricks and craft have put me daft,
They've ta'en me in and a' that,
But clear your decks, and—here's the sex!
I like the jads for a' that.

—*Robert Burns*

A NEW BABY AT THE NEIGHBOR'S

THE SECRET WORLD of women . . .

You call on a neighbor and her new baby.

The house smells of talcum powder and milk and diapers and confusion and love.

The other children come running, eyes big and shining, overflowing with reports and details: "She's got long black hair, just like I had and she weighs eight pounds." . . . "Mommy let me hold her already, and when she gets a little older she's going to let me give her a bath!" . . . "Daddy is *so* proud it's a girl—"

Your friend too regards you with that excited welcome and wonder that is characteristic of someone just returned from some miraculous journey. Her hair is untidy, her figure not yet normal, but she moves with the grace of her own achievement, she smiles with the beauty of one who has glimpsed rare horizons.

"Wait till you see her!" Her voice is touched with a soft marveling pride.

Together you steal to the bassinette, gaze down on the tiny scrap that lies, a hint of pink cheek outlined against the white sheet, a touch of downy black hair.

"How tiny. How adorable—" You exclaim the usual trite but fervent things. "Oh, don't wake her—"

But it must be lifted up, this newcomer, gently raised for exhibiting. "It's time to feed her anyway, and she needs to be changed," the excuse is given. The mother sits down to execute these blessed tasks, ever new, ever strange and special, while the youngsters dance about "helping," enjoining your further adulation. "Isn't she darling? Look at her teensy feet."

And they cast shy hinting glances at the gift you have brought, and are allowed to open it, with much scrambling, and are lavish with their own words of praise. "Mommy, look, just look. Sister, look what you got—a present!"

Your neighbor shoos them out and you sit together a little while discussing it, the whole experience—the secret world of women in which such a thing can be. And you hold the baby a minute yourself, so impossibly tiny, a hot bundle in your arms. Then you hand it back and say good-by, and return to your own domain with memories stirring, and a sense of joy in your heart.

THE RUNAWAY CANOE

YOU REGARD it rocking lightly at the dock, the just-patched and repainted family canoe.

And you feel you simply must assert yourself, if only for the children's future memories. What if they had to recall, "My mother was a hopeless nincompoop. She couldn't even paddle a canoe."

"Come, dear, how'd you like to take a ride?" you invite the littlest, doubtfully.

"You really mean it? Oh, goody, you gonna drive the boat?"

"No, let's not get too ambitious—I'm going to drive the canoe. And put on your lifejacket," you add nervously.

She scrambles eagerly in, grabs a paddle. "Can I help steer?"

"Well, maybe, after I get used to it."

You too step gingerly into the now drunkenly rocking shell, and ease down onto a cushion. "Well—" cheerily, "here we go!"

Fortified by vague recollections of having helped boyfriends paddle canoes in college, you shove off valiantly. But something seems to be wrong. Instead of heading sensibly toward the island, it rears and roots.

"Saaay, lookit Mother!" Your husband hollers from the shore: "You're sitting in the wrong end, honey."

"What difference does that make?" you demand, faintly irked.

"A lot if you expect to get anywhere. Boys, go help her," he orders. And now all the swimmers are regarding your plight and yelling instructions. To your consternation, a little crowd comes sloshing out to hold the craft steady while you stagger to the proper end.

"Go away, go away!" you order angrily as they stand by in an interested huddle. "I can do it."

"Sure you can," your husband says. "Don't watch her. You kids go on and play."

Self-consciously you keep stabbing at the water. "We'll head over to the islands," you inform your passenger confidently.

But the vessel has a stubborn will of its own. Whenever you gee it seems to buck and haw. "I tell you what—" you announce, as the island backs farther away by the minute—"let's go over to the fishing hole instead."

"Okay, I'll help." Your daughter pokes happily at the amiably nibbling waves. With growing confidence you bounce and struggle toward the sufficiently indefinite spot on the silvery platter.

Then a shrill whistle sounds from shore. "Telephone, honey. You're wanted on the phone."

"Okay, I'll turn around, I'll be right there."

But the more fervently you lash the water, the more earnestly the vessel turns its snout toward the opposite bank and dedicates itself to the cause of taking you there.

"Hey, we live over this way, remember?"

"I know, smarty, I know, but it won't *cooperate*."

"Stick your paddle way out and pull back—"

"Turn it a little as you stroke—" "Try the opposite side—" Everybody wants to get into the act. Calling directions, the kids streak down the sand. And somebody suggests brightly, "Get out and shove."

Thoroughly flustered now and mad at the whole bunch, you try to do everything they say, only to find yourself tacking more wildly toward the wrong bank.

"Lassie, come home." A witty neighbor has joined the rousing little group.

"Oh, go drown yourself," you mutter. He's the least of your

worries, however. For now, to your horror, you realize you are about to be cast up on the lap of total strangers having a cocktail party.

They look up from their float at all the commotion, and even your little girl inquires in troubled tones, "Mother, where we *going?* Do we know those people?"

"We're about to," you sputter, through set teeth. "I—seem to have lost the hang of it," you announce in what you hope are charmingly helpless tones.

"Here, let me help." A handsome male squats on the dock, holds out a hand. "We're neighbors? Won't you join us?"

"Heeeey!" Bewildered shouts still echo from the opposite bank. "What's the big idea? Where you going? Hey, telephone!"

THOSE PASSIONATE PERFUMES

To ME, one of the craziest things that has ever happened to an innocent bit of femininity like perfume is the way today's scents are named. To leaf through any magazine bearing the ads of their manufacturers is to run a course that sounds about as sexy as *True Confessions:*

Shocking . . . Possession . . . Love Me . . . Desire . . . My Sin . . . Intimate . . .

All this came to mind the other morning, cutting roses in the garden. Their petals were soft and pink as a baby's skin. The dew sparkled on their cups like crystal, clean and shining, and they filled the air with such a delicate yet heady essence it was sheer perfume. And I remembered my mother's dressing table filled with its exquisite bottles . . .

Attar of Roses, wasn't that her favorite scent? And there was Lilac, Heliotrope, Lily of the Valley. For in those days a name good enough for a flower was good enough for a perfume.

But now perfumes are named after passions . . . Cutting a long-stemmed beauty I held it close and breathed deep. The most ex-

pensive bottle I own could not improve upon that fragrance which
was and is and always will be pure glorious Rose. Yet if those roses
were distilled and bottled they too would promptly lose their
virtue.

Scarlet Letter, they'd probably be called . . . Or Feverish Embrace . . . Or Crimson Crime.

A DAY DOWNTOWN

How WONDERFULLY GOOD it is to get out of the house and go
shopping after being tied down for a long time with small fry.
What a great big glorious world it seems.

Just to see women walking along in skirts instead of slacks, and
with hats upon their heads instead of scarves. To glimpse the latest fashions being worn, and realize with a little smack of surprise
that women are truly women instead of merely trash-toters, grocery buyers, cooks, nursemaids, and domesticated machines . . .

And to gaze upon the wealth in windows and stores. Such jewelry, such furs, such flowers, paintings, all exquisitely displayed.
And oh, such table settings, colorful and charming, with arrangements of glass fruit and candles and mats that give you inspiration
for table settings of your own.

And the furniture arrangements—now why didn't you think of
that idea? A dry sink banked with potted plants sitting gaily before
a window draped with gingham that you could just as well duplicate. You scurry into the dress goods department in search of the
same gingham, and there see a dazzling cocktail suit that you
could also copy on the trusty sewing machine.

How wonderfully good to meet a friend on this excursion, and
have lunch in the dining room. The silver, the linen, the soft
music. And the steaming shrimp and mushrooms—what a welcome respite from a baloney sandwich gulped while perched on a
kitchen stool.

And to be actually waited on by people who act as if they were born solely to serve you. Never suspecting, poor dears, that your usual role at this time of day is wiping noses, refereeing battles, and dispensing peanut butter and jelly sandwiches. For this hour, at least, you are poised, relaxed, chic. For this precious, signal hour you are a queen.

And then at last to go home with your packages, that you spill all over the sofa as you relate the day's activities. Whom you saw and what you did and the bargains you found. And the youngsters dance around you, elated and marveling. For you have brought them more than sweaters and jeans and T-shirts on sale. You are giving them a personality refreshed, revitalized, stimulated. A new self that is heightened and is even made prettier by that simple thing, a trip downtown!

JUST TO PAINT A TABLE

SOME OF US wouldn't shy so at the labors of life if it weren't for the preparations.

You decide to paint a table. But first, your husband reminds you, you're obliged to scrub it down and sand it. "But why?" you plead. "Since it's only going to be all covered up."

To which he patiently explains the obvious: "So that it'll look nicer in the end. Of course, if you don't want to do a good job—"

Naturally that clinches it. What might have been a happy hour's achievement becomes an arduous Project.

But even if you have the good sense to do what painting you're inspired to when a man is safely off the premises, there is still no escaping a long, petty but painful obstacle course of preparations.

You've either got to have the paint already, or go to the store and buy it. Usually you spend half an hour rooting through half dried-up cans. Then you have to find something with which to pry loose the lids. The screwdriver is best, if at hand, which of course it never is. A kitchen knife snaps off, and a nail is too blunt. Finally, you run down the screwdriver (in the sandbox where an offspring was using it to fix a dump truck), free the resistant force, and are faced with the problem of trying to find something to stir it with.

Another trip to the yard produces a few sticks, which are likewise too brittle and break. And the only thing you can wrest from the woodbox is too thick. Feeling guilty, you sneak a kitchen spoon (a deed that would cause family excommunication for anyone else), begin hopefully to dig at the gummy crust, and ultimately to mix and blend.

Meanwhile, you realize that you've got to spread papers down and do something about a brush. Your husband is really very sweet about cleaning out the brushes you invariably leave to harden. But of late, once he's restored them to some semblance of life through long loving soaks in various mixtures, he's taken to hiding them.

The last time he had them cached away behind the furnace; another time underneath the tool chest. After a long maddening search you give up, and stamp feverishly through the children's rooms. At last something resembling a paintbrush is found in a can of red enamel where a son has been working on a Cub Scout tomahawk. It's warped and crusted, however (why *won't* they learn to wash their brushes *out?*), and when you've scrubbed it with various concoctions and dip it gingerly into your sunshine yellow, its red blood spills and its black whiskers fall out.

Nearly frantic with frustration, you begin to yank out drawers, and lo! The numerous fates that have conspired to thwart you have changed their minds. For here is a lush new packet of paintbrushes—all shapes and sizes. Take your pick.

Now at last, blissfully, you are prepared to paint. But after a few blithe strokes the drippings remind you—oh, my goodness, you'd better spread the newspapers. So you grab several from the stack the Brownies are saving for their drive, and open them up, spotting at once several vitally important articles you'd missed. And by the time you've finished reading them there on your knees, the telephone rings. Bikes buzz up the driveway. Doors slam, dogs bark, the kids are home.

And who can possibly paint a table *now?* Better leave it for your husband. After all, it would be a shame to cheat him out of all those other silly preparations.

A WOMAN IN THE SPRING

A WOMAN'S MOODS are subject to the changing seasons. Especially do women relate in some mysterious fashion to the burgeoning earth in spring.

The heart is stirred within us at the scent of growing things. The pulse responds. Subtly, deep in our beings, we feel that a secret is about to be revealed. Some core of truth that only a woman could fathom, some mystery akin to all creation . . .

And a woman feels a restlessness, a giddy, inexplicable aching in the spring. Old hopes rise from a long, long sleeping. For a little while, watching the buds break, hearing the birds' bright promise, we feel them stirring gloriously too—our young, forsaken dreams.

And oh, how we miss people in the spring. Such small things will quicken the image of the loved one lost or merely away. Sunlight on new green grass, the smell of lilacs, a spade on the garden path, a battered hat . . . How they surge back at such moments— mother, father, sister, friend. Or a child. A daughter whose brown legs used to run so lightly down the steps, her soft hair flying. A son whom the wars have claimed . . .

A woman's heart always breaks a little in the spring. But spring offers its own ways of healing. Hoe the row a little deeper. Kneel on the ground and dig the roots. Gather armfuls of bright yellow flowers. Or take the house apart and put it back together shining clean.

THE GREAT GLASSES HUNT

IT FINALLY COMES to all of us—that time when it seems that
books and newspapers are using smaller print, and they're shrinking the eyes in needles. You find yourself holding your work
farther and farther from you, and making the trite complaint, "It's
not my eyes, just that my arms aren't long enough."

Ultimately you yield to the inevitable and wind up with a pair
of "reading glasses." Now practically nobody sits reading all day,
which brings you eyeball to eyeball with a grave decision: Will it
be bifocals, or the take 'em off and lose 'em kind?

If you're the average, red-blooded American female (who'll admit being the mother of grown children, but never to being a
day over twenty-nine) you are *not* likely to buy the kind of half-
spectacles that made Ben Franklin famous. Thus, having been
chief sleuth for all missing caps, gloves, homework, keys, and PTA
notices, you yourself now become a contributor to the store of
things-that-can't-be-found.

The only alternative is to buy and attach one of those chain
things to the elusive lens. However, this too gets a stranglehold
on glamor, and literally hangs it by the neck. Also, the noose
proves a nuisance. The glasses keep bumping into things. Or you
spill cocoa on them. Or the contraption springs the bows when,
in excitement, you snatch them on or off.

After the third set of frames in as many months, I went back
to the old routine of the glasses hunt. Now the familiar cry, "Has
anybody seen my glasses?" echoes through the house. Having one
pair for each floor doesn't help much. It's too easy, when you take
off the ones you're wearing, simply to transport them with you to
some other usually illogical spot. And it's maddening to realize
that at least two pair are hiding out on the same level.

My glasses have been found reposing on paint cans, in and under beds, behind catsup bottles, amidst baskets of laundry about

to be sorted, in bags destined for Goodwill. Once I chased a truck halfway down the block and made them stop and let me go through a half reupholstered chair—and sure enough, there were my glasses.

Usually glasses disappear just when you need them most: When you have to write a check for a C.O.D.; or mend a last-minute tear in a skirt for a daughter whose school bus is appearing around the corner; or catch a plane for distant parts. Then the whole family flies into frenetic search, fanning out to cover the house inch by inch, like a squad of volunteers hunting down a lost child. It's usually the husband's eagle eye which spots them in some appallingly obvious place.

"Here they are, right where you *put* them," he makes his inevitable, if redundant presentation speech.

Generally you're too relieved to respond, "But of course they're where I put them. It's just that somebody always hides or makes me forget the *putting place!*"

TIMES WHEN WOMEN WEEP

LIFE is not all pleasure for a woman. Far from it. There are times when women weep:

When children are seriously ill . . .

When the burdens of housekeeping seem simply overpowering . . .

When money problems seem insoluble . . .

When there is estrangement between fathers and daughters or sons . . .

When in-laws all seem to be against you . . .

When you're tired, half-sick, and discouraged, and it seems nobody loves you at all. Times when even a husband can't understand . . .

No, there are times when it's *not* fun to be a woman. When, like a child, you want to hide in a corner, or run frantically away, or bury your head on your arms and simply weep your burdens dry.

Crying may be a childish outlet but it is sometimes a very good thing. We often rise cleansed and refreshed by the storm. And while it's usually wrong to subject the family to these outbursts, there are even times when a sudden, rare but brimming bucket of tears from that mostly stoic soul, Mother, is good for everyone.

INVENTORY

IT'S EASY so much of the time to feel sorry for ourselves. But the good days we mostly take for granted. Now and then it's fun to take inventory of the things we *aren't* at the moment miserable about. To wit:

I don't hurt, ache, or feel even mildly ill anywhere . . .

I can't think of any pressing problem to worry about . . .

I'm not mad at anybody and can't think of anybody who might be mad at me . . .

The children are well . . .

My husband is well . . .

I haven't pulled any bad bloopers recently to be blaming myself for . . .

I'm not too far behind on my duties . . .

I don't feel guilty . . .

I guess I must be happy!

CONCERTMASTER, MOTHER

ALMOST EVERY WOMAN goes through life moved by a constant chorus of things clamoring to be done.

Her house or apartment is a perennial stage set for this ceaseless background chant—beds begging to be made, tables to be cleared, dishes to be put away, sinks to be scrubbed, papers and magazines to be straightened, clothes to be sorted, ironed, hung up.

All this, not counting the tasks beyond her doors—the marketing, the committees, the meetings, the dental appointments, and such lessons as dancing, music, horseback riding, painting, judo, guitar for her young. Or, if she has a yard—garden chores. There too things creep, crawl, leap, spawn, and toss their green and tattered heads pleading to be hoed and dug and transplanted and fed and mowed and pruned.

She is a kind of concertmaster who can never coordinate, never create any real lasting harmony between all these aggressive, yet appallingly patient voices (they will always wait for her, they never give up). There is simply no controlling or subduing them to a point where they all conclude on time, however desperately she dances from one section to another, waving her broom or trowel or iron. And when she drops spent into her bed, she can hear them slyly tuning up their instruments or running little scales for tomorrow. Even there, she puts herself through rehearsal:

"Be sure to call the milkman . . . the front steps need scrubbing before Jimmy's teacher comes to see about that pageant for Sunday School . . . and he'll need a clean shirt by Friday . . . and I wonder if Bob got that spray for the roses—which would be nice on the platform if the beetles don't eat them first . . . and I'll have to bake a cake for the refreshments—remember to get vanilla when I drop Lucy off for tennis . . . and will my blue linen be okay to wear for the reception?" So that she is for a little while in her mind creating at least one little segment of song that makes a totality, however divergent its various elements.

Thus, when Jimmy has marched onstage to pleasant applause and she in her blue linen is serving cake at the reception, with a rose on her shoulder and more on the table, and the teacher is saying, "He did so well, and you have such a pleasant home," then, perchance, she is aware of it. If only for a minute. It's a little thrill of accomplishment, one small but memorable melody within the eternal dissonance of living.

TIPS FOR A GLOOMY DAY

YOUR HAIR'S A MESS and the house is another. The children are cross and the sun won't shine. In fact, the whole earth seems to have taken on a veil, a gray one, sad and forlorn.

The easiest thing to do is to give up, give in, wrap the selfsame woeful veil about you—and in so doing, lose forever out of life's bright store, one whole irretrievable day.

Instead, why not try to beat those blues? Here are some suggestions guaranteed to help:

1. Put on your brightest lipstick. Do something about that messy hair. Wash it, set it, or whack it off if you're so inspired.

2. Get out of that sloppy outfit, hop into something comfortable that also makes you feel lithe and nimble and gay.

3. Let the children take over one room they can't hurt too much, and there make as big a mess as they like with blunt scissors, finger paints, old magazines, and toys.

4. Whip through the rest of the house as if company were coming and you had to make at least the surface appealing, even if you have to dump things into drawers and behind closet doors.

5. Go into that sodden gray dripping yard and try to scare up a few bright branches, break off a handful of laurel, a chunk of ivy, a few truant flowers.

6. Build a crackling fire.

7. Feed the offspring by themselves and resettle them for naps or play. Then get yourself something really tasty for lunch and use your favorite dishes. Better yet, invite a friend.

8. If the friend can't make it for lunch, have her in for coffee later in the day.

9. Do something you've really been wanting to—curl up with a new book, paint a picture, dye your hair.

10. Put your favorite music on the record player so you can hear it while you work, whether symphony or rock 'n roll.

With a little effort and imagination, that dreary dullard of a day can be rescued and rejuvenated. Try it and see!

THE SECRET OF STAYING YOUNG

"ACT YOUR AGE," we're traditionally admonished. And there are those who ridicule efforts to hang onto at least the appearance of youth.

"No hair dyes for me," women will often say smugly. "And if I'm fat, so what? You don't catch me starving to try and look like the girl I was when I married."

As for men, the male who actually watches his waistline, considers touching up his hair, or investing in a toupee is considered not only absurd, but somewhat suspect.

Yet isn't the desire to look young a healthy, happy thing? Doesn't it relate to the new, the hopeful, the strong, the vigorous, the affirmative in life? Psychologists tell us that action precedes emotion. As we behave, our glands respond.

A youthful look is, therefore, more often than not, linked to a youthful *outlook*. And the man or woman who thinks young even feels young. His step is light, his body usually agile. He is less prone to the aches and pains and illnesses that plague the human species as the years accumulate.

True, we can't all stay sixteen forever. Perish the prospect! Perpetual immaturity would be intolerable. Growth brings not only mental and spiritual rewards, but its own form of beauty. Yet surely this beauty is far more discernible in the woman who is actively interested in beauty. Who refuses to be resigned to the dowdy, the dull, the colorless, the obviously "matronly."

Yet there are those who—quite consciously, I believe—begin to talk old, think old, even walk old, once they reach the middle-age mark. Sometimes they refer to themselves as "the old man," or their mates as, "the old lady."

I believe with all my heart that this is folly, and those who do so are actively encouraging their own downhill slump. Once we lose touch with the dreams and delights and outward manifestations of youth, we are courting age, and ultimately—death itself.

And while age and death must come inevitably to all of us, it is a healthier, happier, and more constructive thing to cling to the best aspects of our youth as long as we can—for to do so is vigorously to cling to life!

RESOURCEFUL SPECIMEN, WOMAN

How TOUGH and sturdy is the stuff of which a modern American mother must be made.

Her resources must be endless; her physical stamina rival that of the ancient Amazons; her emotions (however subject to trial and temporary explosions) basically shatterproof.

How is it that she can rise from her sleep night after night, sometimes for weeks, to attend sick children, comfort one who's frightened from a bad dream, feed babies, cover those who've kicked the covers off, counsel one who's come in late and wants to talk—and still go cheerfully about her labors by day?

How is it that she can make and serve hot cocoa for school patrols on a nippy morning, help with the health program, serve as a lunchroom mother, shepherd a bunch of Brownies to a concert, cook dinner for her family, supervise homework, call people on her PTA committee, and hostess another committee for her husband's club—sometimes all on the same day?

How is it that not only her body but her emotions are able to withstand so many blows and upheavals and remain intact, if not exactly serene? That she can be worried sick about one child's cough, another child's grades, have a stormy fracas with a son about a car, a misunderstanding with a neighbor, a disappointment in the mail—and yet powder her nose, don a perky hat, and go to a charity luncheon where, if called upon, she can rise and make a convincing little speech?

For all the gadgets that have simplified her laundry, her cleaning, and her cooking, the demands upon her time, her temper, and her sheer physical energy have multiplied. She herself is one of the marvels of our streamlined age—a kind of pre-packaged combination public servant and private attendant to numerous other human beings; a keen, efficient, resilient quick-mix of tenderness and strength which today's family and today's society have come to accept and depend upon quite as much as we do planes or cars.

A NEW HAIRDO

NOTHING more seriously affects a woman's personality than the state or the style of her hair.

To the complete mystification of men who are either less emotionally linked to the state of their pates, more efficient in shampooing arrangements, or less vocal about it, any one of us is likely to burst out at any time, "I've simply got to do something about this hair. I can't stand it another minute!"

Whereupon we drop whatever we're doing and dash from the room. Sometimes to the telephone to make an appointment, sometimes to the bathroom to wash the offending mop.

No matter who attends to the matter, in the very act of being sudsed and ducked and rinsed until we squeak, we are purged of many of the minor miseries that beset us.

In the shearing of our craggy locks we are trimmed of at least a few of our trials.

Even in the curling that makes us resemble monsters, there is the temporary illusion of having our problems neatly skewered into place.

A woman's hairdo also has a genuine influence on her sense of well-being. Each of us nurtures a secret image of herself—be it clean-cut career woman, gracious hostess, sultry siren, or just plain Mrs. Suburbia, mother of four.

Imagine then the dismay when the gal who fancies herself a

flirt emerges from the dryer resembling, instead, a stable matron with neatly waved blue hair. Or the career woman who wants to remain severe gets a load of herself in the mirror with a frisky poodle cut.

Such mistakes are sufficient to shatter a psyche. . . . On the other hand, stuck in the rut of a certain hair style (that we may fancy expresses the real Inner-I), we can be catapulted into an exciting new creature by some change we finally are reckless enough to try.

Men escape all this. Their hair types are straight, curly, or bald, and they have practically no choice either way. Except for the big decision as to whether or not to get a crewcut, they usually are stuck with one hairdo for life.

Small wonder then that they regard our harried, hairum-scarum doings with a slightly puzzled eye.

A WOMAN'S VOICE

"HER VOICE was ever soft, gentle and low," wrote Shakespeare—"An excellent thing in woman."

An excellent thing, indeed. Especially when that woman is mother or teacher, for these are the voices that guide and shape the lives of children; their immediate effect is powerful and their influence may last a lifetime.

Think back a minute; remember: Which teachers spring most fondly to mind? Those whose tongues scolded and clacked and clattered? Those who shrieked and railed? Or those who managed to keep order through the quiet dignity of their own presence, enhanced by the voice itself?

Dewey Deal, eighth grade English—will I ever forget that deep, rich voice, so darkly royal it was like walking on velvet rugs. Or Miss Heflin, home economics, whose sweet, flutelike tones sang out above the machines on which we struggled to sew a straight seam. Or in college, Essie May Hill, who had a chuckle in her throat, a joyous, bubbling spring even explaining the Pleistocene Age.

Voices . . . Voices in the schoolroom, voices in the home.

A child awakes in the morning—is it to a pleasant greeting, or a screaming tirade? Which is most likely to set a happy, healthy tenor for his day?

A child eats, goes off to school or play—what is his accompaniment as he goes about these things? A firm but quiet voice chatting, admonishing, advising—or a constant harangue punctuated by outbursts so loud, so coarse, at times so uncontrolled that if it weren't his mother one might think the woman insane. But no, it is only his mother, and though he flinches as from a blow, or scurries guiltily to correct his infraction, or merely becomes inured to it and pays no attention, there is a mark on his spirit, nonetheless. These scars go deep, psychologists tell us, and do their damage unseen.

It's hard not to yell at children, especially when they are small and the problems of housekeeping (or schoolteaching), the budget, and a dozen outside emotional factors are complex. Upon their hapless heads it is all too easy for a woman to vent her disappointments and frustrations, her own sheer weariness.

Yet they are so helpless and small to be the victims of what is actually cruelty. However we try to justify it, to shrug it off, it is exactly that.

In fairness, most women don't *want* to be the harpies we often sound. It is mostly a matter of habit. Of self-control. Of getting oneself firmly in hand. Of practice—yes, and of prayer.

A young mother told me, "I'd hate myself so when they were asleep. I've actually gotten down on my knees beside a crib and cried. And since I was there anyway, I asked for help. And I'm getting it.

"I've learned to keep my voice down, to speak so quietly it's almost funny—they've got to pay attention to hear. And now when I hear a woman screaming at her children, I think, 'Oh, don't. It sounds so hideous to them, to your neighbors, to your husband—and if you'll just listen a minute—to yourself.'"

. . . Her voice was ever soft, gentle and low, an excellent thing in woman.

THE TENDER TRAP OF MARRIAGE

NOT LONG AGO a single woman said to me: "When I was younger I used to regret not being married. There is a kind of stigma attached to being a so-called old maid. Though my married friends were sweet about it, and though I had turned down several proposals in order to stay at my career, the inference was that I'd been left out.

"But now that I'm older and have made a success of my work, I find myself feeling sorry for them. So many of them are frustrated intellectually. None of them are free to travel as I do, and few of them have any independence about money, however well off their husbands may be.

"Sure, they have what's called companionship, but I notice that it's often a pretty hectic kind, filled with noise and confusion and arguments. I notice too that they're forever having problems, if not with their husbands, with their children. Taking a good long look at it, it seems to me the price you pay for being married is misery."

Before such telling arguments what can a mere matron say? In fact, looking at such women from the dusty drudgery of housework or the depths of the very troubles she cites, these arguments sometimes come unbidden. Along with the realization that she herself may have married for all the wrong reasons: Prestige, security, infatuation, a romantic notion of living happily ever after.

But once involved in this "tender trap," she is no longer an individual whose wants and desires come first. She is a wife, a mother, and though she may balk at the sacrifice sometimes and weep copious tears of self-pity, if she's any kind of a woman at all she gradually ripens and deepens in the very process of coping with all these other people and their problems whom marriage has somehow dumped on her soul's doorstep. Poor though she may be in material things, in trips and intellectual contacts, she is rich in the substance of living. A substance which nourishes even as it depletes.

She is rich in responsibilities which, however burdensome, she would not care to miss: The knowledge of being vital to the welfare and happiness of others. Of hearing a small boy yelling, "Mother, Mother, where are you?" when he comes banging in from school. Of frightened voices summoning her to a bedside at night. Of voices pleading for her counsel or guidance over the telephone . . . She is rich in secrets shared, confidences grave or amusing. Rich in a thousand and one opportunities to comfort, share, rescue, direct, and shape other lives.

The wife and mother knows that, for all her disappointments and discomforts, she is deeply cared about. She knows that when she is ill or absent the wheels of the family well nigh stop. She knows that if anything should happen to her she would be tragically missed. More important, she knows that in that instance she will have left behind something valid and significant in the whole scheme of human affairs. People of her own creating, without whom the world would not be the same.

Above all, right now, today, she is caught up in a strenuous but stimulating tide. She is heart-deep in living. Living that sometimes hurts but that is full and meaningful and good.

Little Small Young Things

All my life I've been tagged and trailed
By little small young things, both boys and girls;
Kittens and chipmunks and rabbits that ailed,
And birds to be doctored for broken wings,
And limp little blind fallen squirrels—

—M.H.

HOW DO YOU BURP A SQUIRREL?

WHAT is this chattering as you come up the walk? What is this hopping and jumping and switching of skirts and book bags and ponytails?

"A squirrel, a squirrel!" they inform you as, puzzled, you push through the little flock. "We found it on the playground and the teacher's been letting us feed it all day."

"And I'm the one that's s'posed to keep it overnight," your daughter proudly announces. "And you're s'posed to feed it every half an hour."

The cage, leaking grasses, is carried into the kitchen. Milk from a tiny carton (left over from their morning milk break) is warmed, and one cradles the scared little quaking creature while another pokes an eyedropper into its mouth.

"Not so far, not so hard, he can't suck it!"

"He's not supposed to suck it, silly, you're supposed to squirt it in."

"Here, I know how, let me!" . . . "No, me, it's my turn. Here, Christopher, come to Judy—"

"Christopher?" you ask.

"Yes, we put all these names on the board and voted. Wasn't it lucky Miss Meyer already had a cage? And we covered him with this old red sweater from Lost and Found."

The corps of little nurses keeps busy till time to disperse. Never has one squirrel gorged so much milk from so many. "Dear, are you *sure* it has to be fed so often?" you inquire as squirrel belches begin to disturb the dinner hour.

"Oh, yes, the science department said so. My goodness, it's time for some more!"

By bedtime Christopher is not only bulging, he has practically passed out. Except for continuing hiccoughs he lies inert on his grass nest, eyes glazed.

"Don't anybody worry, I'll get up with him," the eight-year-old announces, though her brother valiantly volunteers for the night shift. "Let's see, how d'you set the alarm clock for every half hour?"

"Every half hour nothing," you declare. "What this guy needs is a little rest from so much Tender Loving Care."

Over anguished protests she settles down. "But I'm *responsible*," she warns. "I promised the whole room I'd bring him back tomorrow!"

Of this fact you and your husband are only too well aware. He is gazing at the still limp if hiccoughing Christopher when you come down.

"Poor little thing, sounds like he's got the colic. Maybe a hot water bottle would help; it does with babies."

"If he'd just stop making that noise. Sounds like he's needing some relief for sure. Say, how d'you suppose you burp a squirrel?"

"Same as with babies, I guess."

Laughing, your partner lifts the little charge to his shoulder and begins to stroke it. With all the anxiety of fond parents, you listen for the welcome blast. To your delight it comes at last, and in a few minutes Chris is curled up fast asleep on a hot water bottle.

At dawn you hear the alarm clock the little one has slyly set. "Gee, I hope it lived through the night," your husband sits up to mumble as heels go pattering downstairs.

In a few minutes you hear a happy tap at the door. "Boy, was he hungry! I think I'll stay up now—remember he's supposed to be fed every half an hour!"

SPOOKY

"No, NO, we have enough trouble without a dog!"

"But the children, dear—and these people have a litter of Labradors—"

The debate wages lively, but who always wins? Mother yields. Mother herself drives into the country to view the candidates.

The first time this occurred in our family, I blush to admit my ignorance. Labrador retrievers, I'd gathered from my husband, were hunting dogs. Which to me connoted a picture of a beautiful white creature standing in profile, one paw raised.

I remember distinct dismay at seeing the jet black mother and her two remaining offspring. "This is the gentler of the two," the owner said. "See, she's a little scarred—the others have picked on her, but the marks will soon go away."

How shy, that quaking black bundle. How scared. And to compound her terror, Ornery, the cat, who was king of the household, dominated her shamelessly until they learned to play.

Perhaps that's why we loved her so, to start. I'll never forget how the six-year-old, whose birthday surprise she was, swept her into his arms, face working. And without a word, strode off down the street with her to show his friends. Or the sight of that little black face bobbing babylike over his shoulder.

Spooky, we called her. And within the year she was satin-sleek and tall. She loved to swim in the stream that flowed by us, and that was fine. She loved to chase the ducks, however, and neighbors' cats and squirrels. She was desperately contrite when caught; she would hide her face in her paws, or squirm frantically under a chair.

She shadowed the children everywhere, but was never one to cavort with other dogs. There was something exclusive about her; when a fellow canine would approach, she would rise and move haughtily away. She was gentle; like a well-bred woman, she spoke only when necessary.

Yet let a doubtful stranger come up the walk, or a sound disturb the night, and her cockles would rise, she would growl, and with three short barks give warning. I could wheel the baby's carriage into the sun and know that this four-legged nurse would faithfully keep vigil.

Three times she had babies of her own. Each time we planned to supervise her nuptials, but invariably some suitor got there first. The first time, we took her carefully to the kennels, and had the "purebreds" all spoken for.

On Mother's Day morning, appropriately, we heard the exciting whimper of new life in the basement. And the whole family rose and tiptoed down. "Stand back," my husband said, flashing a light on the nest. And we'll never forget his gasp, half of amusement, half dismay. "Well, they're *not* Labrador retrievers!"

She loved them, however, her babies of many hues, and so did we. And after that it didn't matter. The household was lively with puppies, and with children begging them. And we gave them all away.

How healthy she was, how strong. We fed her anything and everything and she thrived. Almost her only contact with a veterinarian was when we boarded her during vacations. And these were the only times she ever grew ill—from grieving.

But nature does not vouchsafe a dog the long life man can enjoy. By ten Spooky's sleek black jowls were frosted with gray. When she was past eleven, she suffered a stroke. The tail still wagged mightily, but she was inclined to veer and had difficulty breathing. The doctor did what he could, and night after night we got up to try to make her comfortable.

But finally her misery was too much for those who loved her to bear. We delivered her into kind hands that would gently put her to sleep.

Bidding a loyal dog good-by is a strange experience. It is saying good-by, as well, to a long, memory-filled phase of your family's life. That, too, is why you cry.

TO CATCH A BAT

"Mom, where you keep your paper sacks? Big ones that'll come down over our ears—"

"What for?"

"We're going bat hunting, me'n Johnny, and man, we sure don't want 'em to get in our hair."

"If they did you'd be bats in the belfry," you contribute the little gem as you hand them the sacks, which they draw fetchingly down almost to their chins.

Clutching their homemade butterfly nets—contrived out of old lace curtains and bent hangers affixed to broomsticks, they dash off to the school playground.

"Those kids actually think they're going to catch some bats," you inform your husband in bemused tones, and settle down on the porch. "It's wonderful the faith children have."

"I'll say." He jerks upright presently, at the sound of wild screams. Pale with fright, you both race down the steps. "We got one, we got one!" They are clutching a twisted net, and at its bottom, making a queer sound, is something black and small and desperate.

"How did you do it?" you both gasp, relieved.

"We threw rocks. They'll dive right down at rocks. Get a jar, quick. First we'll put him in a jar, then we'll make a cage and keep him as a pet. Might even charge people to see him. Daddy, you be the one that puts him in the jar. But be careful," your son warns helpfully. "If that thing gets in your hair—!"

You wince. "If that thing gets in the house—!"

You get a fruit jar from the cupboard, punch holes in the lid. Gingerly, the floundering black bunch is eased from the net to which it wildly clings. The lid is clapped on, all gather round to observe a live bat at close range.

"Eeeee—I don't like it!" the little one squeals, diving her face into your skirt.

It isn't exactly pretty—quite small, very black, with an ugly but pathetic baby face, and hunched up wings.

"Poor little thing," you say. "You've got to let him go, he'll only die if you try to keep him."

Reluctantly persuaded, they race off to exhibit the prize to Johnny's mother, who screams, "Get that thing out of here!" and to disrupt the usual hush of the corner library.

"Aren't bats harmful?" your husband ponders during their absence. "Aren't they supposed to be destroyed?"

"Oh, my no—oh, goodness, they just—haunt houses, I believe."

Presently they come trudging back, flushed with triumph, satisfied.

"You let him out, Mom. We sure don't want any bats in our hair."

Shivering, the bold venturers back away. Watch from a safe distance as, with a not too convincing determination, you walk a few paces into the yard and cautiously unscrew the lid. Holding it at arm's length, you tilt the jar. With a scraping of claws, the small dark body slides out. For a sad instant it lies absolutely still.

"Oh, you poor little thing, are you scared, are you hurt? Fly," you beg as it flops on the grass. "Fly, fly!"

Suddenly up it swoops, so fast you jump back several feet. Cutting graceful arcs, it goes bending and blending into the night.

The small boys regard its going with a sigh. "Well," they inform each other, "we can always say we caught a bat!"

WE LOST OUR MITTENS

SUCH A DEAR LITTLE KITTY he was, warm and fluffy and new, gazing at you with his pointed baby eyes. His mew was a comical yeep, his purr a toy motorboat rumbling. How daintily he would wash himself, and how he would play, patting at dangled string with his new little paws, rolling over and over, nipping at his own bewitching tail.

And now he is lost! You have taken him to the country and brought him out into the sunshine to roll and play and chase things in the grass. And become busy with company and when finally one of you remembers, he has vanished.

Where, kitty, oh where in this vast world of weeds and wilderness and water—where are you hiding? What perils have you perhaps already met?

"Kitty, kitty, kitty—" The whole family takes up the call. "Go find Mittens." Even the dog is dispatched. And with quick understanding, the sensitive black nose goes sniffing along the ground.

"Mittens, Mittens, come back, come home!" Its mistress is a forlorn little figure as she trudges up the road. You run and take her hand. Together you search, off side trails, along banks, calling, calling, with a mounting sense of urgency and despair. And after troubled conferences, take the car, asking neighbors, "Have you seen a little gray kitty with white paws? We call him Mittens, though he's almost too young to know that."

So young and dependent. And evening is coming on. Feeling almost guilty, you finally eat supper, setting out first a bowl of milk, just in case.

But it stands untouched. Even the dog, formerly prone to wolf it down, skirts it, crouches on the floor dejected. Oh, Mittens! You all fan out again, searching, until its owner must be put to bed, distraught. "Oh, it's cold out there, it's lonesome, it's hungry—oh, Mittens, forgive me, please!"

You wake several times in the night, listening. Is there a scratching at the door, the faint tinkling of a little bell? But it's only the wind, and toward morning, the rain. And you can't bear the picture of its wandering, bewildered—and that one little gesture it made, of a white paw lifted as if to test this strange new world. And how is it that such an infinitesimal creature can cause an entire family this terrible sense of responsibility and failure?

Morning, your little girl rushes to the door. But the bowl of milk is there, and the little rug you've put out. Taking up her burden of grief afresh, she swallows her breakfast and gets on her coat.

"I'm going out to look for him now."

"I'll go with you," says her father, and together they set off. And you think—at least she'll have the memory of companionship in her first loss.

At last they return empty-handed. Gravely, she hangs up her wraps. "Mummy, tell me honestly, do you think it will ever come back?"

"Honey, I wish I could."

"But why did it have to happen? Why—why?"

"Because life is like that. We make mistakes. Even when we're big and know better we still make them and things are lost, many things dear to us. Mistakes and loss are a part of the way life is. They come to everybody, honey, and we've got to—accept it."

She still prowls the premises, occasionally calling out, "Kitty, here kitty." But gradually there is a new note in her voice. And after a while you hear her playing with her dolls, even singing. And—thank goodness, you think. We do get over things. That, too, is the way life is.

BOTTOMLESS BELLE

"Chicken bones!" a friend cried the other night as I was about to feed our Dalmatian. "Surely you don't give a valuable dog like that chicken bones?"

He couldn't understand why the whole family burst into laughter. Not until we related the story of Belle. Belle, and her freakish appetite.

She had already been named when we brought her home. And though Belle seemed a dignified, dowager sort of name for such a cunning bundle of squirming black and white polka dots, it stuck. She frolicked about the premises as puppies will, making puddles—and the first assaults on possessions.

Shoes were reduced to a pulp. Crayons she masticated daintily, then swallowed, leaving her jowls colorfully trimmed. She tore into and thoroughly digested the biggest, meatiest, most expensive books. She would eat cigarettes, and then, rather brightly the children thought, the matches to light them with.

Unblanching, even unbelching, she would eat not only her dinner; she would go right ahead and eat her feeding dish.

It was definitely no lack of food, we saw to that. Nor was it a lack of toys of her own—she ate the balls we gave her to play with, the rubber bones and squeaking frogs.

Nor did it help to scold and spank. She would simply gaze back with a comical and bewildered expression in her odd unmatching eyes. For one is an innocent baby blue. The other an impish brown. And the result is a kind of weird, ridiculous blamelessness.

It isn't funny, though. Not when you find her contentedly licking her chops after a meal of your best new sample hat.

In sheer desperation we try to put everything out of reach, as you would for a toddling child. Only this four-legged toddler has thrived so on her depredations she has but to rear up on her hind paws and blithely sweep the desired objects to the floor.

On our son's birthday she celebrated by gulping down an entire baking chicken that had been set out to thaw. It must have gone down whole, for we never found a scrap. In fact, we wouldn't have thought to blame her as we hunted for it, had we not caught her helping herself to the just decorated cake.

"This is nonsense," said the vet. "Get her a muzzle."

Which we did. To her delight, for she promptly ate it off!

"Get her another one," he advised on our second appeal. "And grease it with this stuff. I guarantee she won't like that."

Like it? She loved it. In fact, she found this second juicy morsel of muzzle so tasty, she went nosing around until she found the can of grease itself to lick.

One day our daughter was given pills by her doctor. Five dollars' worth. Belle got to the opened bottle first and downed them every one. When we went to refill the bottle the druggist laughed.

"You know what these pills are for, don't you?" And as we shook our heads—"Appetite stimulants!"

THE TURTLE RAFFLE

TURTLE ROAD, they call it. This place not far from your country cabin where they like to go exploring. And it must be Turtle Suburbia, for they never return with fewer than two of its helmeted residents, and the last time twenty-four.

"Good heavens!" You regard the boxes of clicking, scratching creatures clambering over each other. "You must've scooped the whole village, what are you going to do with them?"

"Race 'em, man. Take 'em back to town and sell them to kids for racers. I figure to get two bits apiece for the fast ones, fifteen cents maybe for the babies."

"Not the *babies!*" The littlest wails and clutches a couple of the unlovable looking reptiles to her bosom. "I get to keep some of the babies for pets."

You nip the ensuing fight in the bud and trust that this enterprise will meet the death of waning enthusiasm you've observed before.

No such luck, however. When you return to civilization, the car is crawling with turtles. At home, the car is demoted to the driveway while the garage becomes a turtle racing stable. Pans of water, dishes of egg, lettuce, stale bacon, and dead flies are daily trotted out to the stolid steeds. And small fry from all over the neighborhood arrive to aid, admire, and take their favorites on trial runs.

Turtles, however, seem to be a commodity few kids care to pay cash for. Even prices shamefully reduced and special two-for-one offers fail to produce the anticipated revenue. Meanwhile, back at the ranch, you and your husband keep reiterating, "You've got to get those monsters out of the garage!"

Then one day the manager of the whole turtillian scheme comes home from school inspired. "We'll have a raffle, sell numbers—"

"Dear"—you hedge, with vague visions of rearing a racketeer—"is that exactly legal?"

"Why, sure," he assures you cheerfully, "churches do it all the time."

He has you there. And after a couple of days working the fifth grade and even the playground, he's richer by forty-six cents. "I figure a penny a chance would make it easier for everybody. And," he adds with a grin, "get rid of the turtles."

He's right. After school at three that day kids of all sizes swarm the yard. The big tycoon holds them at bay while he sends little sister in for a hat and his duplicate set of numbers.

You can't help laughing as you look out. The gamblers to whom you could scarcely give a turtle before, are jumping and shoving against each other in their eagerness to win. Mounted importantly on a box, holding a hat and yelling for silence is your son, while your daughter draws the lucky numbers.

There is considerable argument and confusion, of course. Especially when your littlest one insists on taking her babies and stalking off with them. But the lucky winners trudge triumphantly home in the end.

"Well!" Your son ruefully juggles his take. "Now if I'd just charged two cents a chance. Say, when we going back to the lake? How soon can we go back up Turtle Road?"

PSYCHOLOGY'S NO SOLACE

MOTHERS OF CHILDREN with pets should comb the last remnants of college psychology out of their hair. Ax your Adler, junk your Jung, and forget you ever heard of Dr. Sigmund Freud. Never, but never, listen to anyone who speaks in terms of secret motivations, wish fulfillments, and hidden urges innocently acted out. To do so is to open up ghastly new vistas of soul-searching and futile self-reproach.

For whose fault is it all too often when pets escape? Invariably, yours. Who left the cage ajar enabling the mother of all those newborn hamsters to skip out? You, of course. And if you're the self-analytical type you get to probing:

What in the world made me *do* it? Some hidden urge to punish the children for all those noisy wheels going all night long? Or a martyr complex, maybe? You wonder as you sleepily warm milk for the yapping worm-sized babies and fill the eyedropper for the next feeding. Or—good heavens, the possibility strikes—even some secret urge to become *more* the mother than you already are?

This seems so preposterous that even you laugh in self-derision. But still—!

Or take the late lamented departure of Chipper, the baby squirrel. Remember all the arguments you used when the rescue squad came toting him home? Squirrels had everything from worms to rickets. Little creatures fallen from their nests were hard to raise—much better off if left undisturbed. But they won, as they usually do. And somewhat to your surprise, the little guy thrived, even to leaping nimbly about the house snitching peanuts, or perching on a shoulder.

Who was it decided that he needed some fresh air and sunshine? Who put him on a sunny spot on the porch and then was lured into a lengthy phone conversation? You, you monster! And however you grieve and try to make amends, and justify your intentions—isn't it just possible that deep down in your dire demonic subconscious you *wanted* to lose him in order to vent hostility, dominate, prove them wrong?

And when it comes to the lengthy list of lost cats. . . . The behavior patterns— But don't get started on that. In fact, when it comes to parenthood and pets, better send your psychology back!

THE MOST PRECIOUS MOUSE

"OH, MOMMY, Mommy, come look, come quick, help me catch him—a little gray baby mouse."

"I'll catch him all right—in a trap. It must be him and his family that've messed up the cupboards and nibbled everything in the drawers."

She regards you, innocently appalled. The beginnings of understanding flickering about the small eager face. "Oh, but he's a *nice* mouse, I saw him—he's way too little to do any harm. If we catch him and I can keep him I promise to train him not to hurt *anything*."

"Darling, we couldn't keep him, he's a wild mouse. He belongs in the fields. He just comes into the cabin down the chimney or through a crack."

"But maybe he likes it in here where it's warm and there's all the crumbs. I could make him a little shoe-box house and feed him toast and cheese—" She wheels, shrieking with excitement. "Quick, quick, there he goes, into the bathroom, let's run in and shut the door."

Without reasoning, you are in absurd pursuit. The miniature culprit has ducked behind the shower curtain and is wildly circling the slippery stall. Spurred by fanciful Disneyland visions—Mickey, Minnie, and the Beatrix Potter mouselings, suddenly you too want your little darling to have a mouse of her very own.

But Mickey, or Minnie, or whoever he is, is no "wee sleekit, cowrin tim'rous beastie." When you do finally corner him and cup his tiny trembling satin body in your hands, he pays you off, but good.

"Ouch! Why you little—ingrate." Away he scoots, while you regard, in righteous astonishment, the blood on your finger. "He— *bit* me," you announce. "See, honey, mice don't want to live with people, they want to live with their own mommies."

"Not once he got to know me," she insists mournfully. "I'd have taught him such nice mouse manners. And I was going to call him—" She sighs mightily and gazes wistfully out the window, considering. "Golden Diamond Twinkle Star Mouse—because he would be the most beautiful, precious mouse in the world."

ABSOLUTELY NO MORE CATS

"ABSOLUTELY NO. No more cats!" you say when the striped little stray tries to adopt your family. For so many have been lost or met with misfortune. "We have such bad luck with them and you children always feel so bad."

But she simply won't go away. With a kind of wistful patience she awaits the saucer of milk they slip her, and soon is sleeping on their beds. But she is such a little lady, quiet and well-mannered. Never scratching, like some of her predecessors, and simply ignoring the dog.

You don't suspect her condition until one day your little girl rushes in, ecstatic, the bland-eyed subject in her arms. "Tammy's going to have kittens! A girl just told me, she can tell—no wonder she's been getting so fat!"

"Oh, no!" you protest afresh. But suddenly you too are filled with a great tenderness and rejoicing. And all the family shares it. "No wonder she was so anxious for a home, poor little thing."

Tammy assumes a precious new importance as the days pass. Extra milk now, warmed, and vitamin drops. And at night a box in a closet. "They like a nice dark place to creep into, the pet book says."

She walks with a graceful bulging beauty, and lies down with caution, arranging her burden in the gentle circle of her paws.

Her condition complicates your weekend trips to the country, however. She is so restless en route, crying and pawing at the glass. Holding her, you worry, "Just hope she doesn't have 'em on my lap!"

"Animals usually have their young at night," your husband tells you. "I seem to remember from the farm."

But it is on a Saturday morning at the cabin that the stork of kittyland descends. "She's acting awfully funny, come quick, come quick!"

"Now calm down, honey," you tell the child whose personal pet she is. You rush to where the bewildered would-be mother is racing wildly about, and put her in a box. Your husband carries it to a quiet room and builds a fire to keep her warm.

"She's had her first baby," you return to tell the child who is trembling with excitement. "Would you like to come to see it? Tammy doesn't seem to mind an audience a bit."

Enthralled, she tiptoes down, stares into the box, and asks, "D'you think there'll be any more?"

"First litters are usually small, but she looks as if she might."

You return to your book and your breakfast coffee and she keeps vigil, dashing in every now and then to announce, "Now we can sing the 'Three Little Kittens'! This one's so tiny and black, come see!"

So you go to pay your respects. And later again. And again, until the count is five.

"I'm keeping the black one," she firmly says. "Well then I get the gray one," somebody else pipes up. "I want the tan—"

Your husband looks down at the box with its squirming inhabitants, its proudly drowsing mother, and then with a grin at you: "What was that I heard you saying about no more cats?"

Once upon a Lovely Time

I remember, I remember
The house where I was born,
The little window where the sun
Came peeping in at morn—

— *Thomas Hood*

THE WALK TO SCHOOL

I HAVE ALWAYS FELT SORRY for children who miss the experience of walking to school.

When I was a small town youngster we walked at least a mile each way, whatever the weather. And the distance was fraught with wonder, no matter how familiar its landmarks became.

On certain corners there were magic talismans to be invoked—simply lettering on the sidewalk immortalizing some builder's name. Yet the first one to stamp on them and shout, "Good luck!" was sure to be protected from evil all day.

And there were houses that loomed with significance en route. There was the Flower Lady whose entire yard was a riot of blossoms and who might give you some for teacher if she felt in a generous mood . . .

There was the sheriff's house; he could arrest you and throw you in jail if he chose, the older kids claimed . . . There was the Witch's House, an ancient red brick with cupolas and towers, where a daft old lady lived; she sometimes sang from a window, or scurried out in her little white cap to ask if you'd seen her angels who'd flown off again.

There was the Presbyterian Church with its mighty chimes and clock, and its bubbling drinking fountain . . . There was that whispering treasure house, the public library. On the way home you could stop and borrow exactly two books, no more. But by starting them as you sauntered along, you could have them read by tomorrow and borrow two more.

In the fall there was the scent of apple orchards and the dusty scuff and rattle of fallen leaves. You picked up the loveliest samples, scarlet maple, golden beech, to show your teacher, then pin on a paper to trace.

When the first snow fell, you raced joyously through it, trying to catch the cool lacey flakes on your tongue. Drifts did not deter you. They were an excuse to wade.

Snow and ice held the earth fast most of winter, followed by a miracle when the warm days came. For now the gutters ran wild with the melted waters and sidewalks mirrored an upside-down world of sky and clouds and trees. And gazing down, down, you felt a breathless transporting.

You were one of the five foolish princesses who ran off at night into the world beneath the world and danced their slippers to shreds.

You spied the first robin on your way to school. And the first crocus, and it was news. And there were seedpods to be stepped on; how they squirted. And the fuzz of cottonwoods to catch, and dandelion fluff to be blown. And violets to be gathered in a shady wood, and clover to be braided. And you bounced balls, skipped ropes, and raced to join friends who were waiting, or they rushed up to join you. And you argued and philosophized and giggled and dreamed big dreams as you made this daily pilgrimage.

There was time for these things, to think and wonder and truly be a child on these long walks to school.

WHEN FAMILIES READ ALOUD

WHO REMEMBERS a dear and memorable family custom, reading aloud?

In most households fathers did the honors. But in ours it was Mother's role. She had the most beautiful speaking voice in the world, we thought, and she read with "expression."

We were not scholars; few people were in our little Iowa town. No Dickens or Shakespeare or Thackeray for us. We borrowed the popular authors from the public library. Or Dad, taking a stroll downtown after supper, would come home with a striped sack of chocolates from the Candy Kitchen, and a shiny new copy of *The Saturday Evening Post*.

"How about reading to us, Mama?" he would suggest. And heads would fly up from doing homework around the dining room table. "Hurry up, hurry, Mama's going to read!"

The hard-coal burner clucked softly and shed its rosy glow on our faces as we all sprawled around it on the floor.

We gave ourselves over to the spell: Alexander Botts and his Earthworm tractor; the hilarious exploits of Florien Slappey.

Jack London's magnificent stories of the Klondike. The dog stories of Albert Peyson Terhune. Zane Grey's rousing and very pure westerns. Edna Ferber, Kathleen Norris. Gene Stratton Porter's *Freckles* and *Girl of the Limberlost*. Booth Tarkington's *Seventeen*.

We had never seen a real live author and we never expected to. We hadn't the remotest notion of the human beings who labored to give us such delight. To us their names on a book or story were simply tickets to enchantment. They never failed us. That they were not profound never occurred to us. We *enjoyed* them.

They gripped our fancy, transported us into lands and loves and lives more dramatic than our own. Therefore, we loved them. And loved Mother's voice as she sat in the creaking rocker, usually with a sleeping baby on her lap—her voice, the instrument of all this wonder.

Gone, long gone those enthralling hours. Hi-fi and radio and television have drowned out the voices of mere mothers and fathers. Mechanical marvels speak for us. And who needs imagination when everything is acted out for you on a screen?

And even if such were not the case, if all the radios and TVs were suddenly banished, where indeed would the good books be? Can you imagine gathering your kiddies around you for a cozy evening with James Jones or Grace Metalious or John O'Hara?

WHATEVER HAPPENED TO THAT
TWILIGHT TIME?

WHO REMEMBERS WHEN . . .

Children played Run, Sheep, Run, beneath a corner light?

The crowds began gathering right after supper, in that lovely twilight hour just before the streetlamps came on. Fathers had just begun to rock on porches over the evening paper, the smell of their pipes and cigars wafting across the yard to mingle with the fragrance of new-cut lawns.

Mothers joined them shortly, still drying their hands from the dishes; and little girls, with a final swipe at the sink or the kitchen floor tore wildly out to join their brothers, who bossily had already selected their captains and were choosing up sides.

Who remembers the dark breathless thrill of the huddle as signals were decided on? The conspiracy, the plotting, the secret codes.

"Now Tornado Potato means we're going the other direction. But Devil's Pitchfork means we're headed your way, lay low!"

And slipping off across back fences and gardens to hide. And cowering in the darkness, with the stars beginning to blossom overhead . . . the sound of a freight train rumbling through town . . . the lonely barking of dogs. The whole night was mysterious, delicious with danger as footsteps came closer, voices arguing, and your leader called out those signals privy only to you.

Then at last the wild and glorious release of it—"Run, Sheep, Run!" Screaming like banshees you came tearing out of your hiding place, wild horses pounding toward base, not sheeplike at all. For your goal, the sole center of your living, breathing existence, was that serenely shining beacon on the corner, the pale and patient streetlamp.

Who remembers the gnats and mosquitoes swarming there in dinning circles like the children? And the moths that hurled themselves blindly to destruction in that fragile lady's burning eye beneath her scalloped hat. And the great night beetles—June bugs, you called them—fat and shiny, that dropped with horrible plopping clicks, and that the boys would thrust down your back if they suspected your revulsion.

Who remembers the parental voices calling for you to come in now? Insistent enemy orders that you pleaded with in vain. And the slow sweaty trudge back to your own porch steps, panting, tired, but too exhilarated to go to bed. And the cold blessing of a cup of well water, or a glass of your mother's tart iced lemonade.

KITES, OLD AND NEW

THEY BUY THEM at the dime store now, in frail and slender oblongs, the kites that you used to fashion, kneeling with brothers and sisters on the kitchen floor. Is their pleasure the less for the simplified putting together? You wonder, as in a scant five minutes the kites are made.

"The string, where's some string? Oh, goodness, we forgot to get any kite string."

"Nonsense, who needs kite string?" you demand, producing plain white wrapping cord from a kitchen drawer.

"Mom, you can't fly kites with that, it's too heavy," the whole tribe hoots.

"Yes, you can. We always did. Now get busy and help me tie all the ends together."

Grudgingly, with a certain wry bemusement, they obey, and at least one flimsy kite acquires a lengthy launching cord. The littlest (likeliest victim) gets her coat, and to prove your point you accompany her into the yard. "Run, now run," you order, "unrolling the ball."

Excitedly, she obeys. A brisk breeze cooperatively snatches the kite, does its utmost. It wavers, struggles, almost makes it, flops to the ground.

"We told you the string's too heavy," the older ones insist. "That's all the matter is. You've *gotta* have lighter *string*."

"That's nonsense," you stubbornly claim. "Just a silly idea you kids have to spend more money. You think you have to buy everything these days."

To prove it, you grab the contrary little winged ship and plow frantically across the lawn. Again, like a feeble bird trying its wings, it struggles, flails the air, and shamefully falls.

Someone meanwhile has gone to the drugstore. Several fine new balls of kite cord emerge from a paper sack. (No string!) No one bothers to argue. The remaining fleet is efficiently attached and soon soaring.

"Well, I guess you win," you admit with a grin.

Your eyes follow the strange triumphant sails growing smaller above the trees. Your heart feels the old excited tug. For whether it be store-bought or fashioned in a kitchen, whether its cords be thriftily pieced together or unwound from a ball, a kite is always a mystery and a marvel, no matter what one's age.

HOW THOSE CEREALS HAVE CHANGED

WHO REMEMBERS WHEN breakfast cereals were blessedly few?

At our house there was little choice; we got the cheapest—cornflakes or oatmeal. But nothing tasted better than those crisp golden flakes spilling into a bowl, or the oatmeal laced with raisins and brown sugar on a cold winter's morning. Especially if you got "First of the milk!" which everybody started yelling almost as soon as he popped out of bed.

For that was before homogenization and cartons of Half-and-Half in the grocery store. The cream rose like rich furry neckpieces on the throats of those cold but pleasant ladies, the milk bottles on the porch.

On Sundays and special occasions we got shredded wheat or the puffed kinds that were beginning to be sold. But whatever the kind, the cereal boxes sat on the table to be thoughtfully studied while you munched. Though mothers sometimes got fancy and yanked them off, especially when company came, those cereal boxes on the family breakfast table were an American commonplace.

Small fry learned their letters from them; little jokes and games and puzzles could be made. Recognizing this, the companies began to print the jokes and games and puzzles. And soon thereafter the amazing offers which have led the modern American parent to the brink of nervous prostration, beset by youngsters tearing the tops off these boxes, fighting furiously to root out the prizes, and meanwhile spilling their contents all over the kitchen floor. Or besieged by them for "only a dollar" to be mailed with the box-top for membership in a secret club of twenty million members, with a sheriff's badge for identification, or a genuine magic ring.

Breakfast cereal companies have become gigantic business empires that often control the destinies of radio and TV stars. And they knock themselves out continually to come up with something new. The jaded appetites of our offspring are tempted by presugared cereals, cereals that taste like chocolate candy, cereals in the shape of the alphabet, space ships, animals at the zoo.

In fact, today's housewife faces such a bewildering battery on the grocery shelves, and is so put upon by the varieties requested, that her head swims. She thinks enviously of her mother, whose income was more limited and whose choices were few and hearty.

WHEN ATTICS WERE IN STYLE

WHAT A PITY, it seems to me, that in this era of ranch houses, so few children have an attic in which to play.

That "storage space" with a pull-down ladder has been made to substitute for what was once a marvelous boon to both mothers and small fry.

"Oh, go to the attic and play," harried parents used to be able to say to noisy offspring on a rainy day. Or, "Please, may we play in the attic?" the youngsters themselves would beg, as a special treat.

What family room, however efficient, or rumpus room, however gay, can offer the adventure, the enchantment, of the attics of yesteryear?

If possible, I would tack an old-fashioned attic onto every modern house. And the specifications would be:

A door that squeaks a little when a child's hands turn the knob. Stairs that are castle-steep and narrow as canyon walls. A window that looks down from the landing like a dusty, slightly scary glass eye . . .

A mellow and slightly eerie smell for this world of just-under-the-roof. Stale and stuffy, yes, but mysterious and promising, with the tang of the rough unpainted lumber that tops the house and is intimate with the sky . . .

Long empty alleys for running and yelling and noisily pounding feet. Dark little cubbies for hiding in. Floors thick enough to muffle the racket. Yet cups and hollows of space to echo the wild fruity music of children's shouts . . .

Secret attic sounds of its own: A squirrel scurrying along the eaves. A tree shaking hands with the shingles. The wind whistling by. And on rainy days the rhythm of drops on the roof, cozy as popping corn.

Many things should, of course, be stored in this attic: Hallowe'en costumes. Easter baskets. Great boxes bulging with bells and tinsel and Christmas trimmings. Flags from the Fourth of July. All the accoutrements of a magical children's calendar that boasts only holidays . . .

And there should be mysterious souvenirs to wonder about: Thick plush photograph albums, fastened with silver clasps. Bundles of ribbon-tied letters. Pressed flowers. Tissue-wrapped locks of hair. A child's own baby clothes . . .

And in this attic too there should be treasures for playing house. Porch furniture. Old bridge lamps. Bedsteads. A grandfather's clock. And for the dressing up, trunks of old hats and evening dresses and fancy shoes . . .

Lucky the child who has such an attic for exploring. Lucky the parents. Every house that really means home should have an attic on top!

MOTHER'S WONDERFUL WISHING BOOK

"Look, children, see what's come in the mail," I summoned my young one day. "A big fat mail-order catalog!"

They rushed up to see what I was so pleased about. And reacted with about as much enthusiasm as if I'd just presented them with a big fat telephone directory. Its plethora of riches failed to impress them; they see all this and more in store windows every day. And who ever heard of sending away for something you haven't both seen and been fervently exhorted to buy on TV? Politely, they listened to my promises that when it got a little older I'd let them cut it up for paper dolls—and escaped.

Somewhat saddened, I stood sniffing its elusive, nostalgic scent of thin inky pages and thick glossy ones, letting myself be whisked back to the days when the arrival of mail-order catalogs signaled spring and fall. Like spying your first robin, or a scarlet maple leaf. *Sears, Roebuck. Montgomery Ward.* What magical names! For if you lived in a small town or out in the country, they brought the whole thrilling world to your door.

This was important in several ways. For those often snowbound, without much choice in merchandise in the few available stores, these vast packages of print and pictures spread before dazzled eyes almost everything known to the needs of man. Entire families were often clothed and outfitted from their pages. Whole houses were furnished by mail—curtains, rugs, parlor set, nickel-plated stove, and even the kitchen sink. But more, the catalog was a source of information, of contact, a glimpse of fabulous people at work and play. It was a springboard for hope, the touchstone of dreams.

To children, its arrival was as if Santa Claus himself had walked in the door. We fought over turns to explore it, lying enrapt on the floor. We spent hours poring over its pages, especially before Christmas, greedily drawing up long impossible lists from the section marked "Toys." Desperately though we yearned, fervently though we believed in the miracle of possessing, I don't think it was the *getting* that really mattered. In these orgies of imagination we were fulfilled.

In the same way we spent thousands of nonexistent dollars fervently filling out discarded blanks as we "ordered" the most expensive items—furniture, jewelry, furs.

Most important of all were the paper dolls. With the advent of a new catalog we were free to race for the scissors and start cutting up the old. Having each chosen a basic beauty, we would then whack off the heads and feet of other models in order to equip her with a wardrobe worthy of a queen. True, the arms were often in curious positions and the garments didn't always fit; no matter, the dolls continued to beam and that was good enough for us.

Again, we would choose someone we wanted to be. Gloria Swanson, Aunt Tressa, the minister, the mayor, a town belle—and hunt until we found a fancied likeness. We then cut out families for them—dolls that suited and matched their real or imagined circles. My brother dubbed these our "Hippity People"—perhaps because of the way they danced across the floor in a breeze or a blast from the hot-air furnace. Each of us picked a corner of the dining room where we set up housekeeping with our chosen family.

They became vitally real to us one long cold winter when we were housebound with a succession of measles, mumps, and chicken pox. Gloria Swanson visited back and forth with Uncle Horace, the minister, the judge's family. Their children went to parties and dances, had weddings, and when one of them got torn in two, had a funeral. (We found everything in the catalog but the casket.) Then one day when the snow was melting, my brother took the lot of them outside for a boat ride. He was gone a long time. Returning, he confessed. The boat had upset and all our Hippity People were drowned. We all cried. Somehow, it spelled the end of our catalog paper dolls. And the beginning of our growing up.

Yet we never outgrew our awed admiration for the beautiful creatures in those books. What grace they had—standing hand on hip as they chatted with each other—what charm, what style. On them even a housedress looked enticing. And the men were so suave and handsome they glorified even a pair of Big Huck overalls. In the never-never land they inhabited there was no dirt, no dishwater, no floors to scrub, no spilled oatmeal. Everyone was radiant, young, enchanting, and it seemed that if only you could obtain their garments for yourself or your parents, somehow your own dull, small everyday world would become enchanting as well. How was it possible to believe otherwise, especially when you read the poetic prose in which they were described?

Though Mother, too, faithfully studied and loved her catalogs, she seldom sent away for things. "It's hard to tell how things really look from a picture," she said. "And besides you can't always be sure they'll fit. Also," she reasoned, "we should support our home-town merchants. They've been good to us." ("Good to us" meant letting us have credit when times were hard.) We found her attitude frustrating in view of this sure-fire magic. She didn't have many clothes, and my sister and I longed to send away and get her a dress.

A dress was simply beyond our means, after weeks of saving, so we decided to settle for a hat. We picked out the prettiest we could find, not a very big hat, but one richly adorned with fruit and flowers. Eagerly we filled out the order blank, stealthily emptying our banks and slipping off to the post office to buy a money order. We could hardly wait. We wanted it in time for Easter. Our suspense was agonizing as the weeks slipped by. Every time she longingly fingered a hat downtown, or spoke about trimming an old one, we were tempted to tell her.

At last the mail truck stopped before our house. As the driver marched up the walk and knocked we thought we would explode. "But we didn't order anything," Mother protested, even as we began to shout: "Surprise! Surprise!" Baffled, she opened the box, lifted it out of the tissue paper, and there it was in all its glory. Even more gorgeous than we had imagined, rosy and shiny, velvet-ribboned, it was a veritable cornucopia of fruit and flowers.

"Oh, my!" Mother exclaimed, looking slightly dismayed. She picked it up gingerly, turning it around on her hand. "This is for *me?*" She'd never worn anything but the plainest of hats; obviously she was almost too overcome with joy to speak.

She went at once to the mirror and put it on, with some difficulty, over her generous mounds of hair. Her hair was her crowning glory. The hat sort of rode on back of it like a ship perched upon a wave. Until that moment it had never occurred to us that the hat might not become her. In our loving dreams she would be transformed before our eyes into a likeness of one of those dream-creatures of the catalog.

Instead, Mother turned to us looking stricken—half sad, half amused. "Oh, girls, girls, it's the most beautiful hat in the world!" she cried, embracing us. "Just wait, I'll curl my hair Saturday night and Sunday I'll have my powder on. It'll look just—fine!"

It did. It almost did. We all complimented her profusely when she was ready for church, and so did her friends when she got there. But something was wrong and we knew it with a queer wrench in the region of our stomachs. It was our first troubled sip of that wry brew, disillusionment. I think we grew up a little that day, as we had on the death of our paper dolls.

Mother loyally wore the hat—how long I don't recall. After a while it didn't look funny on her any more, it simply became a part of her, like her dependable blue crepe dress. When its flowers began to wilt, its fruit to wither, she even doctored them up and wore it some more. She was actually regretful when at last she was forced to abandon it. "I'll never forget this hat," she said, and she spoke for all of us.

I think of it now on that rare occasion when a catalog comes in the mail. I thought of it as I tried to rouse in my children the sense of delight that a catalog used to bring. But a catalog cannot be the passport to wonder to them that it was to us. These children who are so rich in material things that they are desperately poor in the need for make-believe!

No, really to thrill to the magic of a catalog you must live in the country or a little town. And be a pigtailed dreamer in the days when winters were long and lonely . . . and paper dolls came alive, and a hat was truly a Hat to be worn lengthily, head high, by a mother who loved her little girls.

THE TENT SHOW

SOMETIMES, waiting for the curtain to go up at the theater, I remember my first exposure to this magical experience when I was a little girl in Storm Lake, Iowa.

Spring and fall were the most thrilling times of the year, because Sweet's Famous Players came to town for a three-day stand. The brown canvas tent with the scalloped edges would blossom on a lot beside the railroad tracks.

The dazzling limousine of the Sweets was to be seen parked in front of the hotel. And all day long and into the twilight, the wistful, wildly appealing notes of their music wagon would sing up and down the shady streets, making it positive agony if you could not go.

There was the smell of trampled grass as people crowded up to buy their tickets under the striped canvas marquee. Perched in the wooden box selling them would be George D. Sweet himself, a grave and portly man usually wearing a handsome pearl-gray hat and smoking a cigar.

"Hi, G.D.!" those who claimed to know him would call eagerly; and no honor swelled the bosom more than to receive his nod of recognition and be grandly waved in free.

Sometimes it was Mrs. Sweet who reigned, white-haired, diamonds flashing, like some grand duchess of fairyland. She was rich-voiced, rollicking, flattering, but she seldom let anyone in without paying.

We always sat in the bleachers; they were cheaper than the reserved seat chairs, and actually children could see better there. The orchestra would be playing and the actors, already made-up, were selling boxes of candy in which, if you were lucky, you found a number entitling you to a fabulous prize. (Lamps, dishes, jewelry, temptingly displayed and awarded just before the final act.)

The real suspense, however, was to await the curtain's rise. Finally, when you couldn't bear it any longer, the lights would blink, the actors duck backstage, and the curtain roll up on sheer enchantment.

The three-night stand always included a romantic comedy, a serious drama, and a mystery. All very wholesome. If they were truly Broadway hits (we wouldn't have known the difference), as George D. claimed in his flat little curtain speeches, they had been rigorously scoured of sex and ridden of the oaths that pepper such today. In fact, George D. Sweet's was known in the trade as the Sunday School Show.

Mrs. Sweet was the undisputed star. When she swept onstage people rose cheering to their feet. Always a messenger dashed down the aisle with a mass of red roses which she acknowledged, blowing kisses to make the heart soar. Boldly and inevitably she stole the show, especially in character parts with a thick Irish brogue. The only person to whom she gave quarter was her daughter Marjorie, a Shirley Temple of her time, who later went to Broadway, succeeded, and returned during the depression to lend her talents to try and save the show.

People had radios by then, and talking movies. And cars made it easier to get to the city. Crowds were still good, though lacking the enthusiasm that used to greet the little traveling company. And it was harder to get good plays.

The Sweets had always scorned "Tobies," those cheap farces which are easier to produce and cost less in royalties. Now they were reduced to using them. And to Mrs. Sweet's surprise and secret consternation, the audiences loved them. The rowdier the better. It hurt her pride, her belief in people and all that the show had always stood for.

Then one of her worst fears was realized. She had always been passionately afraid of storms, worried lest one of them blow the tent away. During their last season together a tornado not only destroyed the tent but seriously hurt one of the canvas boys. George D. rounded up another tent from a circus, and the show went on. But his wife never got over it. And when George D. himself was killed shortly afterward in a car accident, she sold the show.

I have seen many famous actors and actresses since those days. But none has ever created the spell of Mrs. George D. No moment has ever equaled that when she received those roses, or the grip on the heart when the Great George D. quietly stepped before the curtain to wish us good night and farewell.

DOING DISHES WITH A DAUGHTER

"Goody, the dishwasher's broken," a daughter said the other day, "now we can wash dishes and talk!"

Wash dishes together and talk, I thought . . . And I remembered the marvelous discussions over the dishes that my mother and sisters and I used to have. The dreams that we dreamed aloud as we washed and dried. And the confidences exchanged. The mistakes, regrets, hopes, ambitions. And oh, the problems to be solved.

There is something about the click of dishes and silver, a kettle of scalding water, a drawerful of fresh dry towels, and a dishpan full of suds . . . Something that breaks down barriers between members of the female sex.

Listen to women working together after a church supper. Or a bunch of women relatives in the kitchen after a family dinner. You can scarcely hear the sound of their labors for the vigorous clatter of their tongues. How they laugh together, consult each other, argue, noisily discuss.

And this is particularly true of a mother and her daughters. The kitchen is a place where they can retreat. They feel safe in its feminine confines.

The stove, the sink, the cupboards—these are eternal symbols of womanhood. And as we scour them, wipe up counters, wash and dry the vessels in which we have cooked and served a family's food, all that is truly womanly in our nature seems to come to the surface.

Dishwashers are wonderful. They simplify immensely the after-meal cleaning up. By whipping the dishes into them at the end of each course the dishes are half finished by the time the meal is done. And even if you wait, one individual—even a child—can do alone what it often took several women working together to achieve.

Yet something else is lost. Something that is meaningful and precious to women: Companionship. The chance—yes, the excuse—to draw together in useful, strictly feminine tasks—and talk.

THE OLD-FASHIONED CHRISTMAS EVE

WHO REMEMBERS small-town Christmas Eves that were always celebrated with a pageant at the church? And the snow that fell so softly, as whole families headed toward this focal point.

Under the corner streetlamps the flakes spun and twinkled like fairies trying their wings. The whole earth wore a jeweled wrap. And your feet made little squeals on the hard-packed walks, like all the voices of excitement clamoring within . . .

The church smelled hot from the furnace. The spicy tang of the tree mingled with that of hymnals and galoshes and coffee brewing somewhere in huge granite pots . . .

Voices hummed, packages rattled, Sunday School teachers frantically assembled children in their proper rows. You swished your head, magnificently kinky from braids unbound, and imagined everybody was thinking how beautiful you were . . .

Shadows moved behind white sheets hung up for curtains. Garbed in bathrobes and turbaned in towels, your father and other men became strangers saying, "Let us go now even unto Bethlehem and see this thing which has come to pass." . . . And the click and swish of the sheets being pulled. And at last the revelation: For there stood Joseph beside a manger with real straw. And Mary cradling a baby—sometimes a big doll, but once a real baby. The minister's new baby! You could hear it crowing and glimpse a moving hand. It lived! For a breathless, rapturous moment, the living breathing Christ Child was right there in your midst.

Who remembers the programs, with their songs and recitations? The desperately pounding heart as you swished forward in your crackling taffeta and new glory of curly hair. The horror of having to be prompted, the triumph of doing well . . .

And the smell of the tiny candles being lighted on the tree, twinkling tallow stars to signal that something magic was about to happen . . . And the jangling of sleighbells in the hall, and the superintendent asking, "What's this? Do I hear somebody?" And the wild and frenzied screaming, "Santa! Santa Claus!"

As you grew older he began to look familiar—like Grandpa Griffith or old Mr. Samsel, or sometimes your dad. But no matter—when he patted you on the head or handed you a bag of hard candies he became the droll elf of the eternal fairy tale of North Pole and Make-Believe.

And the Ladies Aid served cookies and coffee. And parents visited, and children, mad with anticipation, begged to go home for the stockings yet to be hung . . . And at last you all poured out onto the steps that had been paved with ground diamonds.

"Good night, Merry Christmas, come to see us!" voices called as families set off along the cold sparkling streets.

The snow had usually stopped by now. The night was still and clear. All the stars glittered. But there was always one bigger and brighter than the rest. A great gem that seemed to stand still as if to mark the mystery. You gazed at it in wonder all the way home.

MOTHER'S APRON

"OH, MOTHER, buy an apron, please let's buy an apron!" my children urge at church bazaars. Aprons have a special fascination for them; they are forever tugging me toward that table where other women swarm, picking and choosing from among the bright displays. The aprons dancing saucily overhead, or piled in colorful heaps upon the counter. Striped aprons, ruffled aprons, old-fashioned checkered aprons trimmed with rickrack and braid and appliqué. Smart modern ones of orange burlap, hand-painted with abstract designs. A froth of cocktail whimsies of impractical, unwashable net, all bead-and-sequin trimmed.

And suddenly, though an apron's the last thing I want, a little fever of excitement touches me; I too begin to root through this female flower garden and pluck a bright bouquet.

I sometimes wonder why aprons are still so popular, when so few of us actually have much use for them any more? Now there was a good excuse for aprons in our mothers' day. In that blissful pre-cholesterol era hardly anybody broiled or pressure-cooked; no, foods were fried lengthily, smokily, often sputteringly, in good old-fashioned lard. While to bake a cake you coped long and lovingly with flour and eggs and maybe clabbered milk, pausing to shake down the ashes in the old coal range, smash more kindling across your knees, and shovel in more cobs or chunks of rich black dusty coal. An apron was not only part of a woman's uniform, it was protection.

But today, with our instant mixes and frozen foods, only the dedicated cook spends much time in her easy-clean push-button kitchen. And even when she does, her usual costume is shorts or slacks. So who needs an apron?

What inspires us then to make and buy and bestow aprons upon each other, or acquire them for ourselves? Is it mainly that an apron is so—womanly? That apron strings are subtly entangled with childhood memories—the days when mothers stayed home to sew and clean and cook and can. The days when a mother was always *there*.

Women dressed like women then, and anyone who didn't was considered either sinful or slightly cracked. Mothers prepared for their day's assault upon the premises by donning layer upon layer of garments, culminating with a "housedress." A "housedress" might be vaguely pretty, with a bow or a few buttons on it, but mostly it was plain, functional, washable. The costume was crowned with a dustcap, often of sturdy gingham to match the dress. Or it might be a perky concoction of lace and ribbon rosettes. In any case, it protected the hair from the dust that mothers whacked or shook or swept from the house. And always, over all, as a kind of extra fortification, a mother wore an apron. She put it on in the morning and didn't remove it until she cleaned up for the afternoon.

Women were better organized then, perhaps because they had to be. They didn't have cars to whisk them off to meetings or the supermarket while the clothes washed and dried. My mother certainly never did the impulse cleaning to which I'm prone, nor popped a pie in the oven or started an ironing after dark. Each day was sacred to its appointed tasks—the laundry, the baking, the scrubbing; what's more, she arose early, accomplished the scheduled undertaking, and was ready for the sacred rite of making herself presentable by two o'clock. (To be "caught dirty" any time after three would have been sheer disgrace.) This involved at least a sponge bath with a kettle of cistern water heated on the stove, the neat doing up of hair with a number of pins and tortoise shell combs, putting on a "good" dress and silk instead of cotton stockings, finishing off with a touch of rice powder and a dab of cologne. She might receive callers or lie down with the latest installment of a Kathleen Norris serial.

This brief span during the afternoon was the only time she was minus an apron. When she arose to start supper, did she change, as we are wont to, into something comfortable if sloppy? No, indeed, she simply protected her dress with a nice fresh apron. Sometimes a big apron, that encircled her neck like loving arms; sometimes one that tied at the waist in a bow that brothers or your dad would yank when they wanted to tease her. If company was coming, it would be a fancy apron, all organdy frills, the kind women still wear for serving dinners and sociables at the church. But family apron or company apron, it was always crisp and pretty and clean, and she often wore it to the table.

Frequently she continued to wear it on into the evening after the dishes were done. Standing at the back fence visiting with a neighbor, strolling about the yard to see about her flowers, or sitting on the porch in the twilight watching the children catch fireflies. And if the air was chilly, she wrapped her arms in her apron to keep them warm.

It was big enough to shelter you too sometimes if you were cold. There was always a handkerchief for you in one of its roomy pockets. It was a part of her lap.

Her apron gave you assurance. Rushing in from school or play, even if you didn't see or hear her, you felt better just from finding that apron hanging behind the kitchen door or dangling across a chair. Her apron, smelling of cookies and starch and Mother. It comforted you. It made you feel secure. It was a part of her—like her laugh or her eyes or her big black pocketbook.

Sometimes I worry about us a little, we busy, often absent mothers in our slacks. What do we leave behind to greet the child when he comes seeking us? What consoling reminder of our presence?

Maybe that's why our youngsters instinctively want us to own aprons. Lots of aprons. And to wear one now and then. Why we ourselves can't resist buying them at bazaars. Perhaps we still feel the strong sweet tug of apron strings.

Beauty in Your Own Back Yard

Every year of my life I grow more convinced that it is the wisest and best to fix our attention on the beautiful and the good, and dwell as little as possible on the evil and the false.

—*William Cecil*

"SWAN LAKE"

EVEN THE DUCKS can't sleep on nights when the moon is full. Sluggards by day, often drowsing far into the morning with their heads curled under their wings, on moony nights they rouse, making raw little sounds of discovery and agitation. With a stretch of necks and flap of wings, they waddle to the edge of the black satin water and sink into it, to come coasting, like luminous white ghost ships trailing their reflections.

"Look at the ducks," the children say. "They're heading for the moonpath!" And true, they sail directly toward that diamond-riddled bar. Across it they glide, back and forth, tracing their own silvery patterns and making gay, raucous sounds, as if in retort to the frogs in the rushes.

"I'll get some bread." A child streaks bare-legged into the cabin and returns with a bulging sack. "Let me, let me throw some!" Others join her, squatting moon-traced on the float to fling the crusts.

The ducks circle in unison, their movements in such liquid precision that someone remarks, "Swan Lake!" For that is now the picture; they are a quartet of feathered dancers, snow-white, effortless, making their greedy yet graceful arabesques to the music of frogs and crickets and humming night things. While silently flooding the stage from above them the huge round spotlight of the moon shines down.

A NECKLACE OF LANTERNS

YOU BUNDLE the toddler into his bright blue jacket and little peaked cap. "Now let's bell the kitty," you say, and thrust his arms through the red harness with its jingling bells, and turn him loose outdoors.

He kicks delightedly through a pile of dry leaves, laughing to hear them rattle. He squats, hands solemnly on his knees like a little old man, to examine things on the ground.

Industriously he fills his shiny green dump truck with sticks and leaves. Then, yawning, he sprawls sidewise in his little painted chair, cheeks as rosy as the leaves, chin wet and drooling, eyes the bland contented blue of the sky.

The October breeze catches the cold wet sheets you are hanging on the line. Leaves fall, and trees keep up a gentle undulating dance of branches, like old people nodding their heads in resignation as the children leave home.

The little one trots up, rises to futile tiptoe as he grasps for the fluttering sheets. Ah, the fat bulging clothespin bag is nearer. Fingers go probing, discover the fascinating shapes. Vigorously he hurls them from him—into the leaf pile, into the stream.

"Hey, you!" You rush to the rescue—and turn to find him happily straddling the clothes props for a pony ride.

Japanese lanterns hold the sun in orange cups against the white garage. You break off several branches, and some bright-berried stems of a vine. "F'ower!" These too the plump little fists would clutch. Laughing, you string a chain of the flaming lanterns about his neck. They jiggle, delicate and lovely against the vivid blue suit. He laughs too, and grasps them with both hands.

Dumping the whole treasure into your empty basket—baby, berries, and bright fall leaves—you go with a merry jingling into the house.

SQUIRRELS IN THE FALL

THIS IS THE SEASON when the squirrels run freely among the bared branches of the trees.

They are like impish actors cavorting on a stripped stage. All props are gone, no leaves curtain their antics. They chase each other with clownlike abandon, performing their blithe acrobatics unimpeded upon the naked fretwork of the trees.

Their fur is as silvery as the season; their tawny bodies catch the light. They wear their little gray-brown disguises with an air both of blending to their background and of showing off.

Their tails are jaunty question marks. Fluffy plumes.

They are like little ladies waving their fans at a party—or housewives, busy about their marketing. You can almost see them with their shopping baskets on their arms, elbowing and wriggling their way toward the bargains at a supermarket. Then, anxious as parents returning to see about the children, they come scurrying home, sometimes bearing a nut or a bread crust, retrieved or boldly thieved.

Now too their houses are open to behold. Their great leafy nests, shielded all summer, have come plainly into view, rocked securely in the crotches of the trees.

Squirrels are truly free spirits. To watch them running about so lightly, so nimbly, is to feel one's own spirit oddly lifted and heightened, one's own heart lightened and freed.

AUTUMN SHADOWS

SHADOWS come into some new, brilliant individuality on a sparkling day of fall.

Setting off to the store on a bright October morning, you find your own shadow, like the useless imp of Stevenson's poem, tagging gaily yet persistently along behind.

Sidewalks are striped with the inky shadows of your neighbor's picket fence. While farther down the street a steel one meshes the sunlit grass like a woman's hairnet.

The whole neighborhood is wearing a lilting mantilla of shadow-lace. The trees reprint themselves in a shadowy blur upon the pavement.

Nor are they in the least exclusive, these lovely shapes. They sprinkle their charm along back alleys with their trash barrels and heaps of brick. They splay like a fairy fountain across the silvery gray sides of a lumbering garbage truck.

Yet there are strong shadows, too: The long lines of a house lean down to reprint its sturdiness upon the grass. Tree trunks rise in a singing sculpture more powerful than stone.

All the small life of the morning is likewise shadow-linked. A cardinal spurting from the hedge, a bluejay tilting on a branch, a squirrel scampering across a sunny roof, a flock of children playing. Each wears his little shadow as proudly as Peter Pan.

WINTER TREES

TREES are like people. Alike in so many respects, but each so different, so varied, so singular, so strange . . .

This is the season when trees seem to be saying, with that eloquent silence that only trees can assume, "Look, oh look at me."

How their trunks soar upward, strong and joyous with the freedom of boughs uncluttered by leaves. They are like tall-bodied women dancing unclothed in the tingling embrace of sky and wind . . .

And how the branches reach out to admire themselves. How they curve and lift and turn, jut upward, droop low, each in a sculpture unique. Look down any avenue of trees, no matter how similar, and you will find no two the same . . .

Trees stand pure against the sky these days. Only the frail penned pattern of twigs intervenes—and it in a delicate, wispy fashion, as a veil enhances the charm of a woman's face . . .

The trees stand strong, spare, magnificent, and serene.

SNOW COMES BY NIGHT

SNOW COMES BY NIGHT—a quiet magic. A secret tiptoeing down while people sleep.

Only a creaking door, a stirred branch, speak of its coming, and they so hushed and careful it is like the accidental rattle of paper packages on Christmas Eve. Only the outdoors is privy to the snow's secret coming, and it does not reveal the surprise . . .

And now—morning. The first one up in a family cries out, "Why, it snowed last night!" Standing there before the window in excited wonder, he gazes out across the muffled back yard.

The snow lies smooth and untrodden, its white expanse unmarred by any print save perhaps the delicate tracery of a rabbit, as soft and secret as the snow itself. The snow glints with a million little points that grow brighter as the sun rises, as if pleased with itself, growing more bold in its delight.

All the trees are furred with it, the smallest branches bearing their precious ermine carefully against the wind. Now and then glinting veils of it come cascading down, and the trees become graceful dancers, half hidden, half revealed through wheeling draperies.

Snow banks the creek, which flashes along through this white expanse, its black taffeta surface reflecting the sheeted world, and flinging back the light. All its peering rocks wear white fur caps, and its edges are frilled and fluted with ice . . .

Snow comes by night, to fill grown-ups with wonder, and children with enchantment. The youngsters are wild to possess it. They will scarcely eat their breakfasts. They scramble into boots, mittens, scarves. With an urgency and an intentness as instinctive as that of homing birds, they drag their sleds behind them across its white bosom. They fling themselves into its soft yielding flesh. They root and burrow to touch its white heart.

Soon the snow is patterned with their footsteps and the twining, twisting ribbons of their sleds. It is trampled and tumbled and marked up like a scribbled page—but not defiled. For snow is God's own invitation to children, written softly across the world.

THE RAINS OF MARCH

GRAY are the rains of March. Not nimble and prancing with a promise of petals, like April showers. Nor even bearing the soft twining beauty and brilliance of snow. No, they come humbly out of gloomy skies, as if unsure of their welcome or their purpose in falling at all.

They are sometimes but a mist in the eyes of a troubled world, a cloud over its brow. Their tears flow mostly in silence, or softly, as if for sorrows remote but haunting from some far past.

You must listen for their sounds, the whispered sigh, the patient drip from eaves. Only now and then, wind-roused, do they bestir themselves to come battering at the roof in a sudden frenzy, or dancing their dismal dance upon the walks.

Gray are the rains of March, yet paving the streets with silver, mirroring the lights of passing cars, and soaking the trees black as shining knights in suits of mail.

They fill the earth from a vast cup of grief. And it gives back quivering puddles and rivulets that go searching through the old sodden grasses and leaves.

The rains of March are brooding, like a woman bowed with despair. Yet there is a gray beauty in this sorrow, a gentle giving over to temporary despondency. All is not hopeless and lost, this too will pass—we know, we know—but meanwhile let us weep what we must.

SUDDENLY IT'S SPRING

SPRING comes as subtly as snow in the night. It slips up on you with its vague powderings of green.

The maple trees, naked and wind-tossed one day, the next are beaded with buds and standing like princesses serene. In a few more, the tiny, half-seen pricks, no bigger than pencil points, have swollen and become a mass of rosy near-bloom.

The ground is suddenly brash with grass, the forsythias leap into yellow flame. Their fires are purest gold, like fronds of sunshine congealed, thin as lace. And as swiftly as if a wrap had been tossed across their gray-brown shoulders, the hedges turn green . . .

And now the maples begin to rain down their rosy blossoming until the ground is carpeted pink. One day you take your work onto an upstairs porch where the sky is a blinding blue, and you are sheltered by the arched arms of the trees. And as you labor, the rosy bud-flowers keep falling . . . falling . . . with a soft whisper upon your white papers, in a fuzzy plopping rain, like caterpillars . . .

Then, but a day or two later, only the finest, lower fronds of these rosy bud-flowers remain. Above them, like white-green candles, proudly jut the tight-curled leaves.

THE SPARKLERS

THREE LITTLE GIRLS at bedtime suddenly remember they haven't burned all their sparklers, hoarded ever since the Fourth of July. Clambering out of their bunks at your country cabin, they come pleading to be allowed to finish off the fireworks then and there.

Their faces are rosy from too much sun and water; their noses and cheeks clownlike with white dabs of healing cream. They wear shorty pajamas made in an old-fashioned bloomer style, and their long hair is in their eyes.

Finding no objection, you shepherd them down to the patio where a tiny new moon is shining, little and young and thin like a fledgling girl herself. You strike matches and cup your hands against the breeze, to light their precious sticks.

Squealing and chattering, in tune with the creatures that chirp and squeak from the trees, they begin to prance joyfully about, waving wands of brilliance. They are unreal in the pallid light, like figures out of a medieval fairy tale. Not quite child and not quite witch and not quite sprite, with their blowing hair, their curious garb. Their merrily dabbed faces are grotesque in the glow of their sputtering stars.

"Wheee . . . wheeee . . . !" Their voices blend with the night birds' screech. Behind them is the recitative of crickets and locusts, the heavy thunk-thug . . . thunk-thug of frogs in the rushes. The wind tosses the streaming hair of the willows along the bank, and the strands of hair across their glittering eyes.

ANGLING FOR THE MOON

EVERYBODY ELSE is going to have fat-dripping hamburgers for supper, but your husband, who's on a diet, must settle for something harboring fewer calories.

"I know what, I'll catch you some fish," you announce. "And we'll roast them over the coals after the others have finished."

You fly down to the dock and confidently bait your hook. And sure enough, no sooner has the minnow gone diving into the water than the bobber follows and you pull up a lively bluegill.

"Okay, now go get his brothers," you tell the still vigorous bait. But to no avail. Not another nibble do you get.

Determinedly, you sit on the float facing the cabin porch where the others proceed with their fare. You hear their voices, laughing, arguing. You smell the tangy charcoal smoke that sifts up white against the lilac twilight sky.

The small log house on the hill admires its own face in the olive-green water, and beside it are mirrored the long-limbed trees. They lean there like slender ladies draped in shawls of dark Spanish lace. And one of them wears a great yellow pearl in her hair!

Your line reaches straight into this shimmering loveliness. Each time you withdraw it, it is as if you're about to catch one of these lace-shrouded figures—a curious kind of Spanish mermaid. Or perhaps pull in the very gem itself, round, gold-white, glowing.

At last regretfully you retreat. Bearing your lone fish, you climb back up the rock steps. "Hope you're not very hungry," you tell your patiently waiting mate. "This is all I got—but I almost caught the moon."

HOW BEAUTIFUL IS A FISH

"But who cleans them?" people ask when we wax enthusiastic about all the fish we catch at our cabin on Lake Jackson, Virginia. And I am continually baffled by the number of women who act either amazed or vaguely horrified when I admit that I actually enjoy cleaning fish. I might as well, since the sink is usually full of them, and I just can't bear to see the poor things flopping and gasping about.

Fish don't suffer, some people claim. But unless a fish can personally assure you he doesn't mind choking to death I recommend giving him the benefit of a knife. Having severed the head, you can easily yank out his neat little vitals. You then have a handy pocket in which to get a grip while stripping off the scales.

Men, for some reason, save the head till last. "How would you like to have somebody stick a finger down your throat and skin you alive?" you scold. But they insist a fish doesn't feel a thing; in fact he lies so still it could be he likes it.

Techniques aside, our fish are so beautiful. The crappies, the bass, the bluegills. The fat spunky little bluegills especially, armored in gold and silver, with the deep blue scallop behind the eye. And the arched, silver-sheathed crappies. And the heavy yet slender bass, who are a deep olive green yet also a dull luminous gold. Each scale, aligned in lovely precision, is a thin golden coin outlined with a dark pencil. And the dusky green-gold tapers off to the creamy white V of the belly.

When, except while cleaning it, do you really see how exquisitely a fish is made? The pinky tones around the fins and lip and tail. And the eyes, blank, staring, like glass buttons stuck on. To scale a fish is to feel and see a fountain of crystals flying. Or it is like stripping off a sequin sheath and finding beneath it an ever purer, more luminous satin-smooth silver that reproduces the fish's colors and all its markings.

No circus performer in spangles, no princess adorned in the finest fabrics and gems can surpass the sheer shimmering beauty of a humble fish lying in the kitchen sink.

DRAMA IN THE NIGHT

THE DOORBELL rings one night, and a slim helmeted youth informs you you'll be without electricity for a while. "We're working on the transformer across the street."

Instant excitement pervades the house, a sense of impending drama. Candles are brought forth, ancient oil lamps lit. Bathrooms take on strange new shapes and shadows as small fry splash and dry themselves by the eerie light.

"Oh, how beautiful," a daughter calls from the front steps. "Mother, Daddy, come look!" And there it is before you—pageantry and drama on the darkened street.

Crowning the brows of two great throbbing trucks are ruby lights; and from them ruddy fingers jut, painting the wet shining grass with scarlet, sloshing gold on neighboring windowpanes.

Figures move about in this shifting light, purposeful workmen in tropical hats.

Looking curiously like a misplaced professor, one in eyeglasses perches on the curb, bending over a big notebook. A generator churns. From the equipment truck juts a long white arm that bends back upon itself and swings a rectangular "bucket" up and up.

"It's an aerolift," the foreman tells you, a gentle-faced older man who stands arms folded, chewing gum. "Originally used for cherry picking, but ideal for jobs like this. They make them now of fiberglass, which is a non-conductor of electricity."

"Where is everybody?" a neighbor demands, striding from her own dark house. "If it was an accident or a fire there'd be a crowd." And you sit together remarking on human nature that will gather at scenes of catastrophe, yet ignore the drama and beauty of constructive things. And speaking of these humble heroes of the night —men who work at skilled and dangerous jobs, unknown, unsung.

You see the head of the man in the bucket emerge, the thrust of his broad shoulders and his arms, heavily sleeved and gloved as he goes about the intricate task of tackling the ailing transformer. Another man scales the pole and dangles below him, assisting.

Cables are hoisted—lovely shining loops. Like a lean, slightly ungainly monster, the lift maneuvers, shifts. There is a flurry of sparks as wires are cut.

"This I've got to see close up!" You train field glasses on the sweating faces, hard and clean and strong, lit by the casual coals of their cigarettes. They are like the faces of workmen in Grant Wood paintings, the courage and strength enhanced in the shifting scarlet and amber lights.

At length their intricate manipulations cease. The old transformer drops swiftly to the ground. The silvery rectangle of the new is hoisted high. With slow grace the lift with its manned bucket continues to maneuver, the motors to sing and chug. While in the trees insects shrill and scold in a kind of background chorus. Stars flake the sky, dimmed by the dazzling lights.

Astoundingly, it is after two in the morning before the white arm bends back upon itself and gently draws its occupant to the ground. Already, as if life blood has been restored to the dark dead house, the lights spring on.

"Well, we got 'er fixed!" the foreman calls.

BERRYING AT DAWN

YOU ARISE some morning to go berrying at five o'clock. It is still dark as you eat breakfast, so you dawdle over second cups of coffee, watching the coming of the soft creeping pink.

"We can see it better if we turn off the light," your husband says. And sure enough, the room achieves a new personality, mysterious and strange. The windows are rimmed with silver, and in them your jugs of ivy, the pitchers and pots are set out in entrancing silhouette. You marvel over this, and wonder how much of your home you are missing by not getting up to greet it in that cool changing hour when the night is closing shop.

The yard has a damp sweet breath as you open the door; birds are already cheering from the trees. The woods smell minty and wild as you trudge behind your husband along the path. You think of pioneer women who braved dangers with their mates to forage for their young.

"Gee, just look!" Giving shouts of delight at the abundance, you begin to pick. The blackberries glut the bushes, big as walnuts. You have only to stretch out your hand and a wealth is at your fingertips. They are fat and wet and ripe, they rain into your pails at a touch, or plunge into the tangles at your feet.

The brambles tear at your legs as you progress slowly from spot to spot. The sharp fingernails of the vines claw at your hair. You think how lavish nature is with her gifts, and then, sly witch, how she sets up dragons to make them hard to get.

You are conscious of the world beginning to wake. "What time is it?" your husband reluctantly asks. "I really ought to get going to the office, but it's so hard to stop." Finally, gloating over the heaped pails, you tear yourselves away, trudge back along the now sun-bright path.

Your toddler is awake and peering at you from the door, a sopping cherub in a trailing nightgown. He gives a shout of welcome, grabs for the berries and stuffs them into his mouth. He is laughing and purple-chinned as his father tosses him toward the ceiling. Other children trail sleepily in.

"Where you been? Oh, boy, blackberries for breakfast!"

" 'By. See you tonight." Your partner kisses you as you wash and sugar the bright fruit for the children. He too pops a few into his mouth.

"Good-by, we'll have blackberry shortcake for supper." Holding the baby, you wave as he dashes through the bright new morning to the car.

GREATEST DECORATOR

NATURE is the master decorator, but then she has the finest accessories at her command. Curtains and draperies of silvery mists and rain and multihued clouds; the swags and fringe and vivid accents of leaves. And the rugs she unrolls—floral patterns, the lush green of lawns and pastures, the shimmering gold of the fields, or the deep white fur of glittering snow.

There are no discords in nature. An art teacher once called our attention to the fact that in nature colors cannot clash, as they can on canvas or fabrics. For outdoor light has a quality that blends their native loveliness, whatever the hues. Architects finally discovered that the most beautiful, livable houses are those which allow nature to do much of the decorating through windows which frame the landscape and draw the outdoors in.

And in a small, quite amazing way, that decorator, nature, often lends to individuals a helping hand. I used to nag about a rusting oil drum at the lake, which nobody seemed to get around to disposing of. And lo, nature tossed a trumpet vine across it, using it as a trellis for the long lacy leaves, the flowers with their flaming throats. The vine spilled over it with such charming concealment that people remarked on its effectiveness.

And once we lived in an old house where the kitchen window was so close to the stove that curtains would have been a hazard. Yet my husband never seemed to get around to building the scalloped cornice boards I visualized in their place. Then one day the ivy that choked the walls outside came poking through a crack, like a cluster of perky little green faces curious to see what was going on. Before we knew it, they were clambering up the sill and framing it—a living ruffle!

Though a neighbor clucked that such goings-on would ruin the house—that ivy covered up a multitude of sins, both inside and out; and so far as I know the ancient testimonial to good old-fashioned ivy still stands. One thing sure, the finest draperies, the best bought kitchen curtains have never elicited the comment, the admiration, that greeted those gay green "curtains" that nature capriciously decided to hang inside.

THE FORGOTTEN HOUSEKEY

You RUN HOME from a neighbor's gathering on a cool white night. Your heels ring on the silent walks. You turn in at your own and ring the doorbell, for you've forgotten a key. The sound shrills into the darkened house, but there is no response.

You call under your daughter's window and even throw stones. They make a merry rattling against the glass, which remains blank and still. You begin to feel foolish and a trifle concerned, though the empty garage tells you your husband is still at his meeting and you know he will soon return.

Meanwhile, you cross the shining, dew-wet grass and gaze down at the stream. The moon pours its milky brilliance the length of the water and gilds the stone bank beyond. It spotlights the still stubbornly healthy roses, the chrysanthemums and other late flowers.

They come alive with a clarity never seen by day. You can almost trace each petal and stem. Your neighbor's house stands stately as a castle, its slate roof silver-shingled, rimmed with the same fairy light.

You walk up and down the banks in your light coat, and feel like a spirit returned. Like a woman taken from home and family who comes back to wander about by moonlight, shut out but still keeping watch over the place and the people she has loved.

The water visits softly with itself as it races past. You hear an occasional car or voice on the neighboring streets that branch up and away. The trees rustle their dry shedding leaves in the silvery light and the breeze.

Presently the burning eyes of another car swing into your own driveway. Your husband springs out, puzzled, and crosses to the place where you stand.

"Good lord, I couldn't imagine what that white prowling figure was! I thought you were a ghost."

"I am a ghost," you tell him. "I'm locked out, so I'm haunting the yard and seeing it all with the ghost-eyes of the moon."

The Family Holidays

By these festival rites, from the age
   that is past,
To the age that is waiting before—

               —*Samuel Gilman*

THANKSGIVING

IT's GOOD to be a woman when your husband and sons come home from the supermarket, staggering under Thanksgiving provender: candy, cheeses, celery leafing from a sack, fresh pineapple, great net bags of apples and oranges.

The kitchen is a wild clutter of pots and pans and mixing bowls. Little boys hover, snitching samples—a hunk of sticky mincemeat, handfuls of nuts and raisins, a finger lick of the spicy pumpkin you're striving to pour into a pie shell. Little girls clamber on kitchen stools to "help" by stirring and spilling and vigorously shaking flour sifters.

Cranberries bounce into a pan. They make a sound of toy bullets popping as they boil. Children beg to be lifted up to see.

Your husband makes a triumphal entry with the turkey, and the rite of preparing it begins. There is the old-fashioned, country-kitchen smell of singed pinfeathers. You scrub the white firm flesh until it's as clean as the baby's skin.

It's traditional that he prepare the dressing; practically a tradition that he can't find the recipe. Finally, he assembles the ingredients with the fussy concern of a Waldorf chef. You rejoice to contribute the sack of dry bread you can never bear to throw out, but never know quite what to do with. Soon the rich odors of sage and onions flavor the air.

You collaborate on the trussing, the anointing with oil, the binding of the wings. Now into the old family faithful, the speckled roaster, and out to the chill back porch, to await its baking hour.

You sleep late, have a lazy breakfast, then rush to get everybody ready for church. You return spiritually refreshed from this gathering with others, which gives focus and meaning to this whole festival of blessings.

The fire feels good after the tingling outdoor air. Your husband mixes a fruity punch. Children dart in and out, to the reechoing order of "Shut the door!" They present you with a bulging sack of pinecones for a centerpiece, and a spray of berries no rosier than their noses. A teen-ager shoos them from underfoot as she helps you open wide the table and spread it with your longest, loveliest cloth.

The fire dances. The wind rattles a shutter. Your big black Labrador growls and cocks a troubled ear. The mad and merry racket of a football game blares through the house.

Fragrances grow richer and more intense, in the dramatic tempo of a play. Lids tap dance beneath their nodding plumes of steam. The turkey is growing nut-brown, and crackles to your fork.

Small fry keep flat-nosed vigil at the window, watching for company. "They're here, they're here!" . . . "I saw them first, I'll open the door—!"

Aprons are whisked off, fires turned lower. "Now, boys—"

Greetings ring out. Relatives and friends swarm in.

"Everything's about ready. Children, wash your hands. Boys, get chairs to the table—"

Loved ones sit down together, bow their heads. "Dear Father, we thank Thee—"

MOTHER'S DAY

"SOMETIMES I wish they'd dispense with Mother's Day," the woman said to the teen-ager. "I know my children love me; I wish they didn't feel they have to go out and spend their money on cards and gifts.

"Then, too, as an adult I love my own mother dearly and enjoy doing things for her, but Mother's Day makes it an obligation. Not because she expects anything or would be hurt if it weren't forthcoming, but because the advertisers have made it almost a must."

The girl looked back with a kind of troubled astonishment. "Why, I suppose," she said, "I just never thought of it like that. I mean from a young person's point of view it's fun. I like buying my mother a gift—especially now that I'm earning my own money. This year I'm getting her a lovely slip and a corsage. I've been thinking about it all week, looking forward to getting paid so that I could."

And suddenly the event falls into new perspective. Why, of course. Mother's Day, like practically every other holiday—is for the children!

The dancing eyes, the secrets. The giggling, "Stay out of my room!" . . . The pot holders woven at school and hidden under a bed . . . The kindergarten's crepe paper carnations.

And a small girl's sly, "Have you got some material I could use? I mean *big* material, big enough for a big person to wear if somebody was going to make that person a dress?" And submitting to being measured around the waist and draped in an ancient rose print you've dug out of the attic. And warning, "Dear, it's pretty hard to make a dress. I mean you ought to be older and have a pattern."

And the blithe reply born out of the miracle of faith and love, "Oh, I don't need any pattern, I can see it in my mind just as plain—how pretty you'll look in this dress." Aghast at this revelation, she claps her hand over her mouth while you pretend not to have heard.

And a son's dragging you to the drugstore to "look around," while he slips proudly up to the cosmetic counter to spend a whole dollar on cologne.

No, there's no out for us. Even the people who originally thought up Mother's Day probably got a greater glow out of it than their mothers. Gazing at the heap of presents, nibbling burned toast eagerly served in bed, many a mother will secretly agree, "It is more blessed to give than to receive."

But her heart will be full, nonetheless. For she in her own way knows the pleasure of giving pleasure—by simply being the object and center of all this.

This is her secret on Mother's Day. This is the part she plays in the sweet conspiracy of love.

FATHER'S DAY

MOMENTS when a woman admires the father of her young:

Sunday mornings when he gathers the littlest ones on his lap or the arms of a chair, and in his own chipper, comic way reads them the funnies . . .

When he tells a worried youngster: "Now don't fret about that test, just go in there and do the best you can." . . .

When he backs up another who's in a jam: "Just tell the truth and you'll be okay. C'mon, I'll go with you to explain." . . .

When, groaning but game, he agrees to take on another office in the Scouts or PTA . . .

When you see him contriving safety devices for windows, scouring the yard for glass or nails, testing new toys for possible hazards, and firmly fixing anything that could go wrong . . .

When you hear his hammer banging away in the basement late at night, building a playhouse for your little girl . . .

When he hastens home from the office early to help with a birthday party . . .

When he adds an extra ten to the check he's sending a child away at school . . .

When he piles not only his own flock but several extras into the car to take to an amusement park. And when their mothers come rushing out with money, he grandly shoos them off . . .

When, dead for sleep, he snoozes fitfully on the davenport, waiting for that teen-age party to be over so he can pick up the kids and drive them home . . .

When you surprise him quietly going through his old suits, and discover he's hoping to make them last another season so that all the rest of you can have new clothes . . .

When you see him laboring over accounts spread across the dining room table, and know that he's striving to keep up the insurance, manage money for college educations, make sound investments for the future, and balance a badly strained budget— and all without causing you too much concern.

They're not glamorous, any of these things. They probably never entered your head when you were canoeing with him in the moonlight, yelling him on to make that winning touchdown, or dancing with him at a prom. But they're the things that really count. The things that fill your heart when that man you married becomes the man you honor on Father's Day.

THE BIG SURPRISE

THE DOOR BANGS and he rushes in from kindergarten, your rosy-nosed, cowlicky beginner, with his shirttail out and one pant leg trailing. "Mother, Mother!" He hunts you down and hurls himself against you, smelling of paste and crayons and little boy. "I got something for you—don't look, don't look."

Frantically he hides it behind his back and squirms away, eyes shining. "It's something we made at school. It's a surprise."

"A surprise? Oh, my goodness, give it to me quick."

"Wellll—it's for a special day, but it isn't that day yet."

"Dear me, well then I guess I'll have to wait."

You feel his eager anxiety wrestling with the problem. Plainly, he can't bear it. "Oh, no, I *think* it's all right to give it to you early. The teacher didn't say. But first you have to guess. It starts with V," he helpfully confides.

"V—V—oh, dear, there aren't many words that start with V. This will be hard. Vinegar—velocipede—"

"I'll give you another hint." He is ecstatic with his superior knowledge, vaguely sorry for you. "Val—val—come on, try."

"Valance—valuable—I'm afraid I'm stuck."

"Give up? Give up? Here, I'll give it to you anyway." Triumphantly he thrusts it at you, the lopsided red heart with its lace paper doily trimming. "It's a *Valentine*."

"Why, it's beautiful, darling. And you made it all yourself?"

"Well, the teacher helped us just a little, but it's my very best coloring and printing." He heaves a long, proud, rather wistful sigh. "It's fun being big enough to make something for somebody, especially when they like it and are *really* surprised!"

LINCOLN WOULD HAVE UNDERSTOOD

"WE'RE off from school today. Boy, am I glad Lincoln was born! Hey, can I go to the movies? There's a neat show, about these bad guys—"

"Bad guys? On Lincoln's Birthday? Oh, honey, no—"

"Yeah, but the good guys always win."

"I know but—how would you like to go downtown?" you suggest on impulse. "How about visiting the Lincoln Memorial?"

"You mean it? Hey, that would be neat, we could take some of the guys." You reel slightly as he begins rattling off the names of half the Cub Scout troop.

You remind him that you don't have the car. "Let's make it just us today."

"None of the other kids? Just you and me?" He exults before this unlikely situation. (For some reason, solitary possession of a mother's company is something highly to be prized.)

But little sister has overheard and climbs purposefully down from the table. "Me, too. I wanta see Aber-ham Lincoln."

"You're too little. You don't know anything about him, you stay home."

"Oh, honey, no she's not. Let's take her."

A slight Civil War ensues. Vanquished, big brother scolds and bosses in compensation all the way downtown. His small blond target sits unresistant, too entranced before the spectacle outside the bus windows to mind.

At last, after numerous transfers and directions from police-men, you approach the great white marble temple rising majestic and serene in the sun.

"Now you gotta be *quiet* in here," the brother warns as you climb the broad white steps.

"Can't I even talk?" asks the little girl clinging to your hand.

"No, you can't."

"Can't I even *whisper?*"

"Don't worry, either of you," you intervene. "It's just a statue, a big white statue of a truly great man."

"But I thought he was buried here," your son exclaims, obvi-ously let down.

You gaze up at the enormous seated figure which seems so very much alive. The eyes, though grave, seem to twinkle as you at-tempt to explain that this isn't a tomb but a shrine. And the small uplifted faces sense the kindliness. The boy relaxes, actually grins. "He sure was a homely man." The little girl looks as if she'd like to climb upon his knees.

"Was he a daddy?"

"Yes, he had several children. He had four sons."

"Didn't he have any little girls?"

"No, but he loved all children. And he freed the slaves."

Other parents and youngsters stand about, gazing up. Cameras click, light bulbs flash. People speak in low tones. You feel the breeze, brisk and cold and clear. Below you the reflecting pool wears a sparkling wrap.

The littlest has lost interest. She goes to try the steps, climb-ing three or four down, three back. But the boy, in his hooded jacket, stands as if transfixed. His lips move. He reads: "In this temple, as in the hearts of the people for whom he saved the onion, the memory of Abraham Lincoln is enshrined forever."

You postpone the correction, though your lips twitch. Abraham Lincoln, who loved jokes and children, would have understood.

THE EASTER EGGS

"WELL, DEAR," your husband says heartily, hieing for the store, "I suppose I ought to get a few extra dozen eggs."

"Couldn't we skip that part this year?" you plead, remembering previous orgies of Easter egg coloring. "Let's settle for the candy kind. That's what they really like best. At least to eat."

"You mean not color any? Why, honey, it wouldn't be Easter unless we did that. I mean—you and I—"

You laugh and say, "Okay, I guess it wouldn't." And you remember how your parents used to stay up half the night playing egg artists with watercolors. And the years you two have perched side by side at kitchen counters dipping those pesky white ovals and tracing names and little messages with crayons and exclaiming over each other's cleverness. And how they always smell so good that you invariably peel a couple and eat them with salt and pepper before you go to bed.

And you guess there is something about an egg; an old-fashioned, elementary, hen-laid egg that has something to do with the basic values of Easter. That reflects its true significance far more than baskets and bunnies and jelly beans ever can. Because, no matter how you fancy it up, there is nothing artificial about an egg.

Maybe that's why, even if they don't eat them, children want to touch them and hold them and work with them, and find them in the nests along with everything else on Easter morning. An egg, like the grass and flowers and birds that have suddenly burst into being all about us, is directly related to life and newness. An egg is the very beginning.

THE FOURTH—AND UNCLE FRANK

THE FOURTH OF JULY is always associated in my mind with Uncle Frank.

He lived in a distant and to us fabulous city, and it seemed appropriate that he come to visit on an occasion of boom and blast and bust. He was a bachelor, which somehow lent him luster. He was enormously fat, but a snappy dresser, given to white vests and pin-striped suits. He wore a derby hat perched jauntily upon his slightly greenish toupee. He had little shining eyes in a ruddy face which fell away into pleats and folds. He had a fat and genial mouth, wrinkled like a prune. In it was always stuck a huge cigar, which strewed ashes down the vast arch of his belly.

He had an oddly dainty, secretive little manner of speaking from the corners of those plump lips, although his voice came out in a glorious cannon boom. He carried a cane, partly to enhance the picture of the potentate descending, partly upon which to lean his massive bulk, squeezing it through doors, or easing it into chairs. His slender frog legs, destined evermore to be parted by his girth, reached down into small feet, elegant in spats and highly polished shoes.

We thought him stupendously rich, involved in big deals—gold mines, oil wells, real estate, and inventions. He was always seething with plans for less-favored members of the family to make a killing. He seemed on the coziest possible terms with the wealthy, the influential; and his voice rang out with such conviction about the state of national affairs that we were certain he must be a power behind the political throne.

The thing that struck straight to the hearts of his nieces and nephews was his astonishing largess. The first thing he did when he had lumbered down the steps of the train or into your house, was to extend one of his great pink paws. Solemnly pumping your hand up and down, he would pay you lavish compliments: "My gracious, what a beautiful child. And smart too, I hear. Say, your folks should be mighty proud!"

And as, dazzled with praise, half numbed by the grip, you withdrew your hand, you always found in it a shiny silver dollar. Not a dime, not a quarter—a whole dollar to be spent drunkenly on pop and candy bars and other madness that afternoon.

He was through with you then; the audience for his sonorous pronouncements on world affairs, his sure-fire schemes, did not include children. Fussily, he would shoo the small fry from the room.

But we always adored him and breathlessly awaited his coming; and when we learned of his death, it was as if some vital force related to fireworks and celebration had gone out.

He didn't leave any money to anyone. He died broke in a spare little rented room. But he left a legacy of bigness and grandness and generosity that I still feel swelling up inside whenever I smell punk and gunpowder and cigars. And when skyrockets go spinning toward the stars—I think of silver dollars, and of Uncle Frank up there, probably selling God a sure-fire scheme!

EVERYBODY GETS IN ON HALLOWE'EN

ALL THROUGH DINNER the eight-year-old pleads desperately, "Can't I go out just a *little* while? I won't do much, just soap windows and stuff, please!"

"What's with this Mischief Night?" your husband frowns. "Tomorrow night's Hallowe'en. Then you can Trick or Treat."

"They get you going and coming," you tell him, echoing the annual confusion. "Some kids go both nights, one to play tricks, the next to ask for treats. Or vice versa."

"Well, not ours. That's no fair," he says sternly, avoiding your eyes. For both of you are remembering the days when All Saints' Eve was a far less civilized event than it is now . . . The thrill of prowling the night in search of excitement or downright devil-

ment . . . The delicious shocks of the morning after as you witnessed the havoc wrought—the outhouses upended, the wagon
wheels on the schoolhouse roof.

Thus the juvenile delinquents of yesterday. But nobody carried
knives then, you rationalize righteously. There wasn't the wide-
spread vandalism and crime there is today. Pranks were simply
that, innocent and free. Still—our parents were just as hard to
convince, even so.

The smaller boy has been echoing every plea. He wriggles with
eagerness. His round eyes shine. He flings down his fork and
dashes to the window to peer out at imaginary spooks. As the
doorbell rings he goes wild, shrieking after the tricksters, who have
already disappeared.

"See?" the older one triumphs. "Other kids are allowed. I tell
you what—" He suddenly becomes earnestly concerned. "Just let
me into the back yard and gimme the hose, I'll squirt everybody
that tries to do damage to our property."

Surreptitiously, you confer in the kitchen. "Let's give them
each a little bag of corn and let them attack a few windows," your
husband suggests. "That's harmless enough. I'll tag along in the
background to see that they don't get into anything else."

"Okay, and I'll call their Sunday School teacher and some of
the neighbors to come out and pretend to be very scared, or very
mad. They'll love that."

Giggling, enamored of their own wickedness, the boys scramble
into their wraps. Clutching their sacks of ammunition, they dash
into the starry night.

"I know what would be fun," says an older sister, beginning to
clear the table. "Let's dress up like ghosts or something and go
out and scare *them*."

You agree. Feeling a silly excitement yourself, you leave the
dishes in the sink and dart upstairs to dig out sheets. Giggling,
possessed by a sense of some impish intrigue, you wrap yourselves.
Then you too steal into the frosty, bonfire-scented outdoors.

Dry leaves make the brittle sound of wrapping paper as you
scuttle through them, to hide behind the trees. The last late flow-

ers send up an acrid tingling. As the small boys and their dad come back, breathless and joyful from their antics, you rise, flapping and moaning.

The boys screech and give elated chase, capturing you at length and ripping aside your disguise. "Why, it's Mommy, it's Sister. Hey, this is a *real fun* Hallowe'en!"

MOTHERS KEEP ALL THESE THINGS

But Mary kept all these things, and pondered them in her heart. (St. Luke)

YOU MAKE your annual pilgrimage to the attic to bring down the decorations from the family Christmas box. The long ropes of tinsel for the tree. The fragile colored balls, a few always shattered. The faded big red stocking that's hung on the front door how many years? The creche and its figures—Baby Jesus in the tiny cradle that the youngest ones love, the wise men, the shepherds—they are getting grubby, you notice, and one of the kneeling camels has lost an ear.

Really, you should replace so many things. Take this stable, just a rough box on which one of the boys nailed a clumsy roof. Or that angel—too big for the scene; an awkward plaster angel your little girl made and painted with watercolors in second grade. Surely you should throw it out—she'd never miss it. You reach for the wastebasket, drop it in. But suddenly, with the compulsion that makes you rush back to the fireplace to rescue their papers or drawings, you haul it forth again. You can't do it. Because, though its creator would never miss her lumpy angel—you would.

Mary kept all these things, and pondered them in her heart—
How many things a mother keeps, you think as you look about . . . Battered little first books. Baby shoes. Scrapbooks stuffed with their pictures and souvenirs. A daughter's first prom dress

. . . Such foolish things that only a mother would cling to. All mothers. Mothers like Mary, who have gone before—and mothers to come.

"Keepsakes," is written on a large box on the shelf. And in it, lovingly labeled by fingers long still, is a yellow sailor suit that belonged to the child who grew up to be your husband. His own first laboriously printed Christmas cards. And his first pair of red boots. His mother, too, kept all these things. When we were first married I used to wonder why. Then I had a child, and I understood.

Mothers keep all these things. Because they are the physical reminders of our children, the shed garments of a time that, however hectic it may be now, will some day seem precious.

Mary kept all these things . . .

You feel a renewed kinship for that girl-mother. You wonder what reminders of His childhood did she perhaps save. His first little garments, or the sandals in which He learned to walk? A wooden toy cart perhaps, that His father had made for him in the carpenter shop? And what memories did they bring back to her later to ponder in her heart?

You take up the bulging box. This year, as usual, its contents will all make the journey into the holiday with the family. The lumpy angel, the battered bells, the beloved red stocking, mended and refurbished with a bright new bow. It wouldn't be Christmas otherwise.

Because Christmas is for keeps. It comes every year and will go on forever. And along with Christmas belong the keepsakes and the customs. Those humble, everyday things that a mother clings to with her hands, and ponders, like Mary, in the secret spaces of her heart.

GOOD-BY, CHRISTMAS TREE

TAKING DOWN THE CHRISTMAS TREE is like stripping the feathers from some beautiful bird. Even the children, so eager to do the adorning, escape this chore if they can. And after a dutiful insistence on a mother's part: "You can at least take the ornaments off the lower branches," and (visualizing havoc): "No, dear, I'd rather you didn't climb the stepladder to get the angel off the top," you shoo the children off, privately relieved. Like many another rite of womanhood, this one seems to be a solitary task.

You go about it with vigor, wrapping the bright baubles and stowing them in their boxes; efficiently winding the prickly strands of tinsel; and, with the probable foolish thriftiness that men seldom understand, plucking the frail silver icicles to save them too —as many as you can. How they dance in the still staunchly shining lights! How they cling to the brittle branches and your hand. Small though their actual value, you feel their growing weight like a tangible treasure that is too precious to throw out.

Too precious. The branches reach out their arms. Even the dry tick of their falling needles does not mitigate the sense of some gentle imploring: "Stay, stay!" And though you yourself have said, in the hectic rush of holiday preparations, "Christmas comes too often. I wish we could just skip it every other year," and, in the chaos of papers and presents, "I'll be glad when we can get out of this mess," now you stand haunted by it. The whole of it, from the very beginning. From your first shocked protest, seeing the decorations and hearing the carols in the stores: "No, no. It can't be Christmas. Not again! Why do they have to start it so early?" to this moment.

For there was scarcely time for Christmas, after all. The shopping, the cards, the baking, the parties, the programs at church and at school. Almost before you knew it, it was Christmas Eve

—and you stand remembering the children's anticipation, so intense it was akin to anguish. And the rattle of wrappings, the squawk of a doll, as you and your husband stuffed stockings, laid out gifts, in the ancient, thrilling parental conspiracy. And the focal point of it all—this lovely tree. Like a queen, the tree graced the window, pouring its rainbow lights upon the snow and welcoming you when you returned from midnight services. And then it was morning, and the youngsters were shouting, "Wake up, wake up! Merry Christmas. Come see!"

How festive it all was, the tree reminds you—the dear, still shining tree. How joyous. Belatedly, you stand there, wanting to stop its plunge into the past. Not let Christmas truly be over—as it will be over and done with, once the tree is down. And with the going of that tree, another year in the life of your family.

Never again will things be just as they are now, with the children just this age. A toddler, a second-grader, a Cub Scout, and a son who has known the thrill of shopping with money from his first paper route. Next year Jimmy will have abandoned his bike for a car, and the daughter who wanted one final doll will be asking for clothes, instead, and be interested in boys.

There will be other gifts, you know, the pleasures and the problems of other stages. But with each passing holiday the children are growing away from you—and, like this tree, will eventually be gone. And you can't wrap their bright, insistent lives in tissue paper and store them in a closet. All you can wrap, to treasure and hold fast, are your memories.

But now, this very Christmas—which you approached with such resistance and found at times so trying. How could I? a mother wonders, standing there alone, gazing at the lights. They are almost more lovely shining on the bare uncluttered branches. Their strings are like living eyes, blinking merrily. Flooding the tree now in scarlet, now turquoise, gold, and a merry fountain of winking hues.

It is time to hush their bright clamor, time to silence and darken their gay reign. Come now, unplug them. Just a touch of the hand. And as you reluctantly reach out, you bid the tree good-by: "It's been wonderful, hasn't it? Why, it's the very best Christmas we've ever had!"

THE FAMILY CALENDAR

THIS IS THE SEASON of calendars. They make their bright bustling invasion even before the old year is laid to rest. Flat in their envelopes, the mailman leaves them, or tightly rolled in cardboard cylinders. Or husbands tote them home in bulging briefcases, and children gather around excitedly, to inspect and admire.

"How d'you like this?" Father asks. A large, impressive one is unveiled, with colored scenes of sailing ships. "Or this one? It hasn't so many pictures, but there's sure lots of space to write dates."

"I want the kitty one!" . . . "Dibs on the one with airplanes." . . . "Hey, no fair. You had that one last year. You take the one with the foreign countries. Use it for geography." . . . "He can't have that one. Daddy already promised me!"

Calendars, you think, taking down the old one in the kitchen, to replace it with the new. And you remember how this same scene was reenacted over and over in the years of your growing up. Big hearty Dad, with the calendars advertising coal, hardware, the barbershop, insurance—and the family eagerly gathering around the dining table.

Were calendars even more profuse in those days—and prettier, you wonder? Or does it only seem so now? Those purple mountains. Those waterfalls. Those Indians. Those cupidlike girls. Women often saved the pictures and framed them. Today, with our gay prints and draperies and mural wallpapers, it would be silly to save a calendar picture.

Yet, with a tinge of regret, you hold it a minute longer. You know it isn't the illustration that makes you reluctant to part with it. It is the scribbled notations: *Surprise party at Engel-bachs'* . . . *Dentist, Johnny, 4:00* . . . *Get box off to Susan* . . . *Mark's wedding* . . . *Graduation* . . . *Cake to PTA.*

Some of the spaces are crammed with appointments and with reminders. Others bear witness to a child's eagerness: MY BIRTH-DAY. (*Pony?! Hint, hint!*) and a picture of the pet he's dreaming of.

It is tattered and smudged, this packet of papers you hold in your hand. It is fingerprinted and jelly-smeared. Yet it is a rich document of living, for fixed there with pencil strokes are all the things that mattered, the occasions so eagerly anticipated: the parties, the plays, the dances. The contests and football games that ended in such glorious triumph, or such defeat. The hopes, the disappointments, the tragedies. Finished now, over—only a few of them to remain alive in memory.

And gazing on the new one, so bright, so clean, unmarked, you ponder: What record will be written there before another year has passed? What shining events to be looked forward to? What trivial tasks dutifully cited; what joys, or sorrows?

For the calendar that hangs in the kitchen is so much more than a sheaf of dates—it is your family's history.

Apron Pocket Philosophy

It's nice to be important, but it's more important to be nice.

—*Old Saying*

SHUT THOSE DOORS BEHIND YOU

"SHUT THE DOOR behind you!" my mother used to remind us as we all came banging in. And, "Shut the door!" I hear myself, like countless other mothers, calling out to my own flock.

Shut it to cut out the draft, the cold—yes, that's generally what we mean. But in the larger sense, those words can be significant. For the habit of shutting doors behind us is invaluable to happiness; we must learn to shut life's doors to cut out the futile wind of past mistakes.

The man or woman you didn't marry. The house you didn't buy. The job you didn't take. That long-gone injury that is so much better forgotten. That loss, that devastating sorrow, that failure.

Forget it. Put it firmly away. To leave the door of memory even a little bit ajar is to provide passage for grief, remorse, regret—a flock of deadly enemies that can only damage the bigger, better, forward-looking people we should be today.

Look ahead. Advance, proceed. Reach out your hand toward the new doors waiting to be opened, the new dreams and opportunities. They are the doors that should concern us, not those through which we've passed along the way.

Shut that door behind you. Lock it and throw away the key. The only doors that matter are those that we open today!

LIVE WITH IT A LITTLE WHILE

"LIVE WITH IT a little while," a dear friend Helen, who stayed with us during the war, used to say. The lamp you weren't quite

sure of, the picture hung in a new spot, the piece of furniture—
"Live with it a little while and see."

And what good advice it proved to be. Because in a day or two
perhaps, a week or so, the answer was usually quite evident. Either
the object had settled down cozily into its surroundings to com-
plement or enhance them, or it jabbed and harried you until one
day you'd exclaim, "I just can't stand that picture leering at me
a moment longer—it's got to go!"

And she'd laugh and agree, "You're right, it just doesn't *do* anything for that corner. Try it somewhere else."

Unfortunately, we can't make the same maneuvers with people,
with a husband or children. Whether children prove to be blessings or little beasts, we're stuck with them.

Even the neighbors have a certain inescapable permanence. I've
never met one yet sufficiently accommodating to pack up and move
somewhere else if it was plain he was never going to *do* anything
for me.

No, there are many things in life that we've got to go right on
living with, regardless. People. Troubles. Problems. But the funny
part about "living with" that which can't be changed, is that we
adjust to them. After a while they don't seem so bad. In fact, we
get so we'd be lost without them.

SERENDIPITY

SERENDIPITY . . .

I had never heard the word until the president of Iowa's Cor-
nell College, Dr. Arland Christ-Janer, used it at an alumi meeting.
Serendipity—finding something better than what you were looking for.

Being a born word-hound, I proceeded to search for it in my
battered dictionary. Then my Thesaurus, which doesn't have it
either. So I called a friend, who rushed over with an armload of
references. And though we never did find the word—there among

her offerings was some rare and wonderful data I'd been madly hunting for an article.

We could only regard each other in amazement—the proof seemed so clear. *Serendipity.*

We take so much in life for granted. We complain so often of its cheatings, denials, shortcomings. Yet actually life is so richly laden a tree that it's almost impossible to reach out to pluck an apple without getting baskets full to overflowing.

College itself, for instance. We go for so many reasons—because it's a status symbol, or an avenue to the professions, or "necessary," they tell us, "in order to get ahead." And lo, the mind awakes, the sheer adventure of knowledge stirs, and off we sometimes gallop on careers undreamed of, or a lifelong love of arts previously unexplored. . . . And the friendships made, particularly with beloved professors.

Two of my own, Toppy Tull, English, and Judge Littell, Political Science, became father figures to an enormous family of students, who form little clans in cities wherever they find each other, so that what began as something casual on a campus has deepened and ripened to something permanently dear.

Serendipity . . . Something better . . . Every commitment that we make holds this built-in potential.

Marriage, which begins with the supreme and sole desire of two people for each other, expands almost inevitably to include children, relatives, friends—love that multiplies in shining circles around this first self-sufficient unity, enhancing and enriching it far beyond its original scheme.

Parenthood is so much more than just "having a baby," which is as far as most couples visualize at first. It involves the whole agony and ecstasy, mystery and marvel of creating and rearing new human beings. And though our offspring seldom fulfill all our first fond specifications, they often so far surpass them later that we are amazed.

Serendipity. It's at work for all of us in large and little ways. Shopping for a dress and finding a whole outfit. Inviting a foreign student for dinner, and finding yourself in turn a guest of the ambassador. Taking a shortcut which turns out to be a longer but far more beautiful way.

Buying a house—whether you seek a spanking new rambler or a crumbling mansion—invariably you get so much more than you bargained for. Headaches, drawbacks, yes, we get those too. But they seldom hold a candle to the unexpected blessings of new friends, church, school—a veritable rainbow of opportunities arching across shining new horizons toward unanticipated pots of gold.

Serendipity. Steadily, all unseen, it's functioning for us every day. Surely it works best for those who are serene enough to receive it. Perhaps that's the secret of its power, as well as the source of its name.

SOLITARY CONTENTMENT

PEACE is a rare experience for a busy wife and mother. Quiet is almost an unknown commodity. Generally the only way to acquire a precious hour of silent solitude is to wait until the entire family is bedded down. Even this takes a bit of doing, and often you're too tired to enjoy it once you succeed.

Or, hopefully, patiently, slyly, you browbeat the young fry through their homework and start the bedtime treks a few minutes early, only to be caught in the net of your connivance: "But it's early yet—I've got to get a bath—I've got another chapter to read—hey, no fair!"

Even on the nights when with luck you succeed and are prayerfully about to settle down, the ensuing quiet may be shattered. Somebody wants another drink of water; somebody else has a nightmare; or, most dismal of all (making you feel a meanie), you are summoned instead to the night nurse shift as a plaintive voice calls out, "I don't feeeel gooood!"

But again—ah, again, somehow the simple, homely, blessed miracle is achieved. They are silent, every last one of them. No voice cries out, no footsteps go pounding along the hall. The house is yours, a strangely changed and promising place in which to do what you will. The hours stretch forth in a soft shining vista, their possibilities limited only by your own endurance.

What first—a bath, a book, or both? First the long sweet soaking, then a book—or a stack of magazines waiting like riches on the coffee table. Or possibly the TV—a late movie or a program to be savored in the sheer luxury of just being alone. It is almost too much, you must taste these pleasures one by one. And so you poke the fire, heat the coffee, turn the set on low, and take up the book, or dip into the enticing stack of unread magazines. Or, if you're so inspired, you uncover the portable typewriter and write long letters to dear ones, or possibly poetry. . . .

The night is all around you, close and comforting. It is like a good friend, someone so understanding it does not intrude but only rests quietly by your side. Its eyes shine through the window, its voice murmurs gently in the whisper of the fire, the breath of the wind.

You are your own person now entirely. For a little while you have escaped all demands. You are your own.

CORDIALITY

OF ALL HUMAN TRAITS, I believe cordiality to be my favorite. That warmth of greeting, that enthusiasm which makes everyone, friend or stranger, feel welcomed, wanted, liked, and enjoyed.

Maybe this is partly because I was lucky enough to grow up neighbors to some people named the Johnsons. What the house lacked in luxuries it more than made up for in this rich quality. You felt it like a gift, a kind of happy bestowal, the minute any one of its members opened the door.

"Well, come in, come in. Say, but it's great to see you—hey, Dad (or Babe or Jack or Lois)—look who's here!"

It made you feel special, that greeting. It made you feel like someone they'd actually been hoping for. Nor did this cozy, glowing sensation leave, no matter how long you stayed. They talked with you, they laughed with you, they focused their attention upon you with interest and warmth and joy. And they never seemed to want you to go. "Ah, come on—listen, you just got here. Wait now, have another cup of coffee, let's talk some more."

That everyone who entered got the same treatment didn't diminish the value of your own reception a bit. You knew, somehow, that they were sincere—they *did* enjoy people. All kinds of people, attractive or not so attractive, rich or poor. Cordiality was not just something assumed out of kindness or courtesy, it was unconscious, spewing naturally out of an innate delight in human fellowship. Therefore you accepted it, trusted it, knew with an overwhelming certitude that, whatever your own shortcomings, you were truly welcome here.

Cordiality . . . Cordially yours . . . It is not a lost art; there are many who still practice it, if only because it's their nature, they can't help it. Yet I wonder sometimes if sheer old-fashioned cordiality hasn't gone out of style? People so seldom sign letters "cordially" any more. The occupants of some homes seem to have lost the hang of it. Despite the perfunctory courtesies, even some of the most excessive attentions, you feel uncomfortable. As if, "I shouldn't have come," or "I mustn't stay long," or "How soon can I politely leave?"

What a pity! Doorbells were meant for ringing. Houses for the entry as well as the departure of visitors. True, often we are so harried, preoccupied with personal concerns, that the unexpected arrival of some caller is not a thing of joy.

And yet . . . if we could only all be Johnsons. Able to sing out, and truly mean it, "Well, come in, come in—look who's here!" And, "Oh, stay just a little while longer, it's so *good* to see you, please don't go." Our own hearts would be the richer.

DON'T BE AFRAID TO BE FRIENDLY

MY FATHER was a bold and jolly man. He "never knew a stranger," as the saying goes. He used to embarrass my mother—in fact all of us—by his habit of addressing people he'd never seen before, on public conveyances, or at fairs and celebrations on the street.

"Nice day, isn't it? Say, this is some crowd." And he would introduce himself and pleasantly ask, "Where you from?"

"'Fools rush in where angels fear to tread,'" my mother would despair of him, shaking her head. But I think she envied and admired his lack of inhibition, for it freed him for rewards not enjoyed by more timid men.

For almost invariably the face would light up, information would be vouchsafed, often an interesting story volunteered. Sometimes for only a few casual moments, but often much longer, he would have made a friend.

"Everybody really likes to talk if he'd just admit it," Dad used to say. "Half the time people are dying for somebody to pay a little attention to them." He would smoke his cigar and chuckle, his bald head shining under the parlor light. "The way I figure it, life would be mighty lonely if there weren't some of us willing to break the ice now and then."

His philosophy makes more sense to me the longer I live. Propriety, good manners, good taste, the fear of being conspicuous, of being rejected, our motives misunderstood—such are the locks behind which too many of us quake, lonely, bored, and too shy to make the first move.

I once rode a hundred miles on a bus beside one of the most fascinating women I have ever met—before either of us had the courage to speak to each other and discover a common interest which kept us talking avidly during the scant half hour that was left. We all have been at cocktail parties where, overwhelmed by numbers, and failing to find a familiar face, we spend a miserable time—until somebody, some total stranger, takes pity on us and speaks. When, by the mere act of introducing ourselves, starting up a conversation, the evening might have been successfully launched. Not only for ourselves, but for someone else.

Shyness is actually a form of selfishness.

HOSTESS TO LIFE

SOMETIMES you think you can't stand the chaos any longer: The telephone's incessant ringing, often before you are out of bed. ("Is Susy there?" . . . "Can you take over lunchroom duty?" A den mother. Your son's piano teacher . . .)

And the errands: Doctor and dental certificates to be signed. Socks to buy while you're near the dime store (how is it humanly possible to lose so many socks?); and a birthday party present— and ribbon, paper, card. The bank, the bakery—and home in time to wash and dry a slip for a daughter to wear to the party . . .

And the deluge after school: "Make me a sandwich, will you? I've got to get back to football practice." . . . "I can't find my trumpet!" . . . "Where's the Scotch tape? Where's the card?" . . . "Wait'll you hear what that mean teacher did today—!" . . . "We're having Scout inspection, I've got to have my uniform pressed and the emblems sewed *exactly* one inch down." . . .

Little folks chasing each other in full cry. A lamp upset. A quarrel settled. Extra kids for dinner (will the meat go around?). More phone calls shattering the meal: "May I please speak to Bill?" . . . A friend apologizing, "I hate to bother you, but did you ever cook venison?" . . . A man about the insurance . . . A dancing studio gaily announcing, "Congratulations. You have just won a free cha-cha course."

Then the wild scramble for TV programs. People shooting in all directions to meetings. More people popping in: The paper boy. A stalled motorist. A prospect for one of the puppies. A neighbor wanting to cut out a rocking horse on your husband's power saw . . .

Papers on the floor. Schoolbooks. Blocks, crayons, a headless doll, a baseball bat. Coke bottles on an end table, pretzels on the piano. The cat whining to be fed. The dog barking. The power saw dimly screaming; every radio and record player going.

Oh, to escape! you sometimes think. Oh, to lead the quiet life of contemplation in the woods—or better yet, a good hotel.

Then the motorist, thanking you for use of the phone, looks about and grins, "This house really looks lived in."

"Lived in is putting it mildly," you agree.

He leaves and you bend to your tasks—straightening things up, turning noises down. And you think about his remark—how right, you realize. For your household is constant host to that priceless thing called *life*.

This is life that flows in and through you, battering you with its demands. You are the channel for the strong, vigorous blood beat of a living family.

And though it fatigues and harasses you, sometimes almost beyond endurance, through it too you are strengthened. It is the tonic that keeps you going. It is your very reason for being.

"NOBODY KNOWS THE TROUBLE I'VE SEEN"

THERE is a popular belief that it's a good thing to talk out our troubles. That it is the quiet, self-contained souls who more often wind up in institutions, because they lack this safety valve for letting off their emotional steam.

Yet women are far too prone to pounce upon this warning and use it as an excuse for pouring out problems to friends, relatives, neighbors, in a continual stream.

Now one close friend may be fine for this purpose. With the kindred spirit who knows us wisely and well, it is sometimes a downright pleasure to disclose our secret selves. The trouble is that many women have too many such seeming soul mates. They run from one to the other being desperately self-revealing. Until suddenly this ceases to perform its original function—the desperately needed outlet—and becomes instead a habitual orgy of self-analysis and shoulder-weeping. And in it the person so beset begins to find greater satisfactions than in quietly meeting and coping with his problems, in salvaging such happiness as he can from life as it is.

Another danger is that in such outpourings the individual refuels his resentments. He recharges the batteries of his misery. He —or more likely she, gets all worked up afresh. Because "Emotion follows action." And it is usually true that the minute we begin to reenact, through recital, the dramas of our woes, the nerves and heartbeat respond, the tears are eager to flow from their abundant well.

Even physically this can do very real damage. It adds to the wrinkles, the pouches under the eyes. While emotionally, what might have begun as a really glowing day turns, because of this sorrowful reenactment, into an exercise in misery . . . Reenactment. It is said that some of those who participated in the Civil War Centennial battles actually got mad all over again at the long dead enemy!

Sometimes that's how it is with us. The enemies—past slights, hurts, betrayals, have long been dead, many of them. Why disinter them? Or if sometimes we must—well, there is always that patient listener and counselor, the pastor. Or, if you can afford one—a psychiatrist.

LOOK OUT—YOUR PUNCTUATION IS SHOWING!

DID YOU EVER think of people as resembling punctuation marks? There is the period person, for instance. His judgments are decisive. His pronouncements final. There's simply no use arguing with him, period. He always has the last word.

Or take the quotation marks personality, who carries on almost his entire life's conversation in quotes. Impressed by his vast reading background, and the rich storehouse into which his retentive memory can dip, you seldom stop to think that he produces almost no ideas of his own.

The comma person is hesitant, meek, and a trifle pedantic. Careful pauses mark his sentences, as if compelled neatly to hook each thought before proceeding.

The colon and semicolon type is first cousin to the common comma, though a bit bigger, broader, often trailing an advanced degree and a Phi Beta Kappa key. His pauses are less those of the uncertain and tentative than of the organized thinker who lovingly groups his often complex ideas. No mad rush of words for him; you can almost see the structure of his concepts impressively laid out.

The CAPITAL LETTER individual Thinks Big, Talks Big. He is a name dropper, and the bigger the Name the better. Yet he is robust and entertaining, for everything he describes is Epic in scope. He can make a trip to the market to buy a pound of liver sound like an African safari; or if female, a polite thank you to the man who picks up her gloves on a bus, the beginning of a mad romance with a VIP.

No use trying to relate *your* adventures to the Capital Letter Kids. They're simply too enthralled with their own, you don't stand a chance. But they can be fascinating.

Then there is the species of human being whose entire approach to life seems to be shaped like a question mark. He concludes his simplest statements with, "Isn't that so?" "How about it?" "Wouldn't you say?" He doesn't converse with you, he tests his ideas on you in a kind of earnest interview. Which can be flattering, of course, but also disconcerting.

The no punctuation at all personality talks a blue streak racing from subject to subject without pausing for breath and seems to have been born talking and will die talking and is hard to get away from especially on the phone but he's often warmhearted and wonderful.

His (or more often her) next of kin is the parenthesis person, who eventually gets *back* to the original idea, but only after wandering down a bewildering labyrinth of side trails. "This was when Arnold was five years old (Arnold, by the way, was my husband's little brother, who'd been adopted by his stepmother, his stepmother was one of the Flying Filberts—did I ever tell you about their act?) Well, it seems—" And eventually, "Now where was I? Oh, yes, Arnold—"

My favorites are those people whose whole approach to life is best expressed by an exclamation point! They have the gift of enthusiasm. To them everything is vital, exciting, stimulating. They are vigorous, not only in their own speech, but the manner in which they listen. They are not afraid to exclaim.

"An exclamation point in writing," said F. Scott Fitzgerald, "is like laughing at your own jokes." Well, me, I like people who laugh at their own jokes. And at other people's. Who aren't ashamed of their own emotions, or unwilling to share yours.

Exclamation mark people! Give us more of them!

PATIENCE

PERHAPS the hardest lesson to learn in life is patience. To wait unperturbed while the child in the highchair does everything with his food except eat it. Quietly to hear out the interminable tales and complaints of the harried neighbor, the long-winded friend, or the very old. To give earnest attention to a son or daughter as he describes in minute detail the movie, or an episode at school.

Not to interrupt. Not to cut the other off. Not to explode. To curb the forces within us that would hurry, hurry, hurry. To hush the frenzied voices of rebellion. To still the frantic and usually

futile impulses that would result only in hurt feelings and unnecessary distress . . .

These few minutes lost—what actually do they amount to in
the long span of living? Are they worth one tantrum? One
wounded spirit? One rejected soul?

True, the baby must be induced to get at least a few bites of
the carrots or spinach down. The son and daughter—yes, they
must be steered back into the course of homework, duties. The
neighbor, the friend, the aged—there are times when somehow
we must have the courage to bring the encounter to an end. But
meanwhile—patience. Patience.

Withdraw the emotions, practice detachment, kindly interest,
self-control. With the conscious effort comes a strange calm, a
sense of being not the prey of outer forces, but in command of
some subtle yet significant inner forces of one's own.

TO TRIUMPH OVER FEAR

WHAT A TRIUMPH it is to overcome the fears and aversions that
beset us. What a sense of self-mastery it gives.

Some things we simply outgrow: Not to be afraid of the dark
any more; nor to fear going into a lonely attic, the hiding place
of ghosts. What a thrill for one child to say to another, "Come
on, I'm not a-scared, nothing'll hurt you—" and to see him take a
friend by the hand and lead him into the place of imagined
threat.

Yet some of us take years to overcome our aversions. As a child
I was once teased with a snake. Thereafter the mere word in a
book was enough to make me skip the passage, a picture was a
horror. Once at the Smithsonian, accidentally finding myself in an
area where the creatures were realistically mounted, it was all I
could do not to bolt the place, screaming.

The first year we summered in the country I lived in constant
misery lest one of these ancient anathemas appear. What's more,

every child was fitted with boots, which he was ordered to wear whenever he set foot outdoors. By the end of the second summer, however, the silly rule had been pretty well forgotten. In the first place it was an unenforceable nuisance, in the second—expensive. Everybody kept outgrowing those high-priced boots. Furthermore, my mortal enemies were so scarce as to be a rarity.

And gradually the subtle miracle of nature had begun to penetrate: Harm does not lurk behind every boulder and blade of grass. Such hazards as it harbors are far less than those of busy city streets, and more than compensated for by its peace and beauty and wonder. If you can't trust it and accept it on those terms then you belong elsewhere.

Meanwhile, the children's enthusiasm for all living things, whether they flew, hopped, swam, or crawled, began to draw me into their world.

The first time our four-year-old came running excitedly up holding a twining length of living ribbon, it was all I could do not to gasp, "Put that horrid thing right down!" But I did not want to curse her with the phobia that had enslaved me. Furthermore, I was stopped by the sheer pleasure on her face.

After that, little by little, the V-shaped silver patterns that an occasional water snake drew in its gentle course became a source of pleasure rather than alarm. I was able to join the family and watch with fascination instead of aversion the behavior of one of them as it engorged a fish. I could not only face a snake book without flinching, I began to study such books, along with the others, so we'd know the poisonous ones when and if they ever came around.

We learned that black snakes are actually friends—they keep down rodents; what's more, harmful snakes for some reason are seldom found in a black snake's territory. So when a fine stout black snake adopted our Point the better part of one summer, it actually added to my sense of security. And when some strangers came along one day and killed it, I was indignant. How dared they destroy "our snake," which we trusted and which had never done anyone harm?

Thus gradually we can overcome some of our deepest aversions. It's a slow process, and takes a combination of both will and willingness to learn. But in the end it spells freedom—and often new enjoyment.

ANTIDOTE FOR MISTAKES

SOMETIMES we think we're the only people who make mistakes. "How stupid of me!" we berate ourselves. "How could I have been such a colossal idiot?"

And we regard, appalled, the extent of our blunders: Expensive purchases that cannot be returned. A seemingly impossible assignment assumed from which there is seemingly no escape. Wrong choices, commitments, decisions that we may be stuck with for years—sometimes for life.

Because, while some mistakes can and will be corrected, to a very large extent most of us have to live with our mistakes. Worse, other people often have to live with them, and it is painful to know that because of our own errors in judgment they too must endure.

And then to our vague surprise and consolation, we discover that we're not the only ones! Other people err too. Often wise and admirable people whose judgments would seem to be infallible.

Dispirited recently over what seemed to be a bumper crop of bloopers, I was heartened to fall into conversation with a learned judge. He was kicking himself all over for a list almost as lengthy as my own: "We bought the wrong house in the wrong neighborhood at the wrong time and there's simply no getting out of it. It's the only place big enough to take care of my wife's parents— and taking them in to live with us was another mistake that can never be undone."

While I was sympathizing with his predicament, my own spirits were curiously assuaged. It isn't alone that misery loves company;

rather that our follies don't seem so abysmal when we are reminded that mistakes are the common lot of man. We all make them. Little ones and big ones. Whatever their size or shape they're pretty much inevitable. And punishing ourselves only compounds the problem. Instead, we should face up to them and make the best of them.

For lurking somewhere in the body of every mistake there are compensations that we find only when we stop scolding ourselves long enough to look for them!

TAKE TIME FOR OLDER PEOPLE

THERE'S A MAN in my life I can't forget. He doesn't know it. He never will—that's what haunts me.

No, he isn't romantic or handsome. Just somebody's grandpa, who was standing in the corridor one day at school. Not a daddy any more, busy about setting up tables for the fair, or there to see about a child's homework. Not president of the PTA, or even a member, just—there. And I should have paused, if only for a second, and said "Hello." Should have found out who his grandchild was, made him feel welcome. But no, I rushed on about my business, and he stands there still in my mind—ignored, lonely, feeling in the way . . .

That's what's so cruel about aging. One day you're racing about the business of life, harried but vital, a part of its machinery. Then gradually but inexorably you are left out, until one day you find the machinery tearing along without you—and nobody even notices. Your worries may be behind you, but so is your importance, your sense of involvement and of having a right to be where the younger people are.

And the younger people ought to remember that we too may be standing bewildered and embarrassed in a school corridor one day . . . Or sitting forgotten in a corner while bubbling young matrons discuss their children or the last dance at the country club. Hoping to participate, to contribute from our rich fund of anecdote or observation—but fearful of intruding. Only nobody bothers to notice.

Actually, elderly people are often fascinating. They're so filled with wisdom and experience. And so gratifyingly pleased when you show an interest in what their lives have been. Older men particularly. One question alone serves to bring light to a retired man's eyes: "What was your profession?"

Before these magic words a man warms, expands, unfolds. His life's work! It may be far behind him, but whatever it was he's usually proud of it: "I was a doctor . . . an accountant . . . I worked for Standard Oil . . . I was a union leader . . . I was an engineer."

And the attention of any woman makes him feel masculine once more. I used always to serve lunch to the old gentleman who tuned our piano, and you never saw anyone so pleased. Once he brought along a comrade from his boardinghouse, and I got out the good silver and made a casserole and warmed them with sherry. There was a sparkle in their step they hadn't had when they came.

How I wish I'd served up at least a friendly word to the man I remember at school.

LIFE TAKES A LITTLE NERVE

WHEN I WAS A CHILD there was a certain girl my parents liked but never really approved because, "She's got such a lot of *nerve*."

I've come to believe, however, that the example of Nicky's nerve —her uninhibited daring before new people, new experiences, was really good for the shyly squelched rest of us. That often fools who rush in where angels fear to flutter get places angels don't.

At least they have a more interesting time of it.

Certainly the simplest achievements of life, as well as the bigger ones take—a little nerve.

It takes nerve for a boy or girl to go out for football, enter a speaking contest, run for class president. A dread of being conspicuous, of "not going over," plus a kind of comfortable laziness keeps many a promising youngster from trying out for the paper, the class play, things they may really long to participate in and have real aptitude for. And this same combination of fear and laziness must be overcome in order to blow the lid off their own talents.

A woman who is today a concert pianist told me that after winning a scholarship in high school she was terrified at the prospect of leaving home, traveling to the distant academy of music. "The mere business of a train trip, of living in a big city appalled me." Only by a desperate summoning of sheer nerve was she able to resist the easier, more comfortable course of simply staying home.

What defeats so many of us is that it's so much easier to give in to the humdrum way of living, not even to try. One day when we lived in a small Texas town, I was enjoying a leisurely breakfast when I read that Dale Carnegie had arrived on a lecture tour. "Why not go down and try for an interview?" something urged me. But the coffee perked enticingly, and after a few hours at the typewriter I was going to play cards with the girls. Why spoil things? I was very young and inexperienced as a writer, he'd probably be too busy to see me. Besides, what would I say?

Yet nerve can be very stubborn sometimes. Dreading the whole thing as a foolish, self-inflicted ordeal, I went. And was not only graciously granted the interview, he hired me to substitute for his regular secretary who was sick, and gave me much valuable material and help.

It takes a little nerve to make friends. To introduce yourself in a new neighborhood, to be first to call greetings across the yard. But it pays fantastic dividends.

It takes a little nerve to be kind sometimes, when being kind also means being conspicuous. Yet one kind word to that lost or lonely stranger can change his day—and quite possibly his life.

Anything worth doing takes a little nerve. If you're one of those bored, "nothing ever happens to me" people, ask yourself if it's simply nerve you lack. Go after that job, that audition, that interview, that friend. Consoling as it is to think that all things come to him who waits, it's a lot more practical and interesting to go after them. Or when opportunity knocks, have enough nerve to open the door!

A Woman and Her Friends

A friend is, as it were, a second self.

— *Cicero*

FRIENDS ARE NOT A
ONE-WAY STREET

A FEW WEEKS AGO in New York an old and valued friend remarked, "I don't bother with anyone who bores me. I have cut down all my contacts to a minimum, I see only those people whom I really enjoy."

With the instantaneous reaction of the very busy I thought for a moment, how wonderful. To have matters so arranged that one would be spared the countless contacts that often seem frantically and futilely time-consuming.

And yet, on reflection, I'm not so sure.

Aren't friendships, on whatever level, a part of human fortune? Friendships can be infinitely varied. And by their very different-ness the whole pattern of one's days can be enlivened, and in so many ways rewarding.

Sift through your friendships; sort them.

There is the rich inner circle of those people who are dearest to the heart. Usually these are the persons to whom we can most honestly express our deepest selves. And even though we may not see them for days, weeks on end—even years—the bond remains strong and special and true.

Yet would we not be the poorer without the infinite variety of others?

Friends can be friends for so many different reasons. There is the wonderfully helpful neighbor who is always willing to give you a hand with the children, or whip up a skirt for you.

There is the witty one who can always make you laugh.

There is the one who sends over bones for the dog, and is generous with praise for your growing crew.

There is the quiet soul who occasionally comes up with a star-tling gem of philosophy.

It takes patience sometimes to appreciate the true values in the people with whom circumstances have surrounded us. It takes awareness to recognize these values when they appear.

Yet almost everyone has something uniquely his own to contribute to our lives—and equally important, a place in his own life that perhaps we alone can satisfy.

The heart has many doors. Don't be too quick to bolt them.

REAL FRIENDS ARE NEVER FAR APART

ONE OF THE SAD IRONIES of our busy metropolitan lives is that the friends we love and most enjoy are often those we seldom see.

In small towns where everybody is your neighbor, your friends are but a few blocks away. You meet them almost daily on Main Street, at church affairs, or PTA.

In cities, however, friends are physically parted for miles. It takes so much effort to get together (what with transportation complications, the problem of baby-sitters, not to mention the sheer strain on the budget that such arrangements entail) that frequently we simply forego the pleasure. Except for a luncheon date in town when both of you have to be there anyway, or a specific dinner invitation, you may go months on end without ever seeing the person your heart may hunger for.

In short, what kindred spirits so often miss through the accident of urban living is spontaneous communion. That quick delight of drawing together when you have exciting news to share; or problems that only this person who loves and understands you can help you solve, if only by lending a sympathetic ear.

Yet one of the compensations of true friendship is that people who are truly congenial *don't* drift apart. Anyone who has traveled very much, or lived in different parts of the country, discovers this. From among all the countless people one knows at each place, there rise to the surface one or two couples or individuals who remain steadfast.

And though time and distance reduce your contacts to perhaps one letter a year, when and if your paths do cross again, you find yourselves excitedly picking up the threads of friendship precisely where you left off. Because what united you in the first place was something that went beyond mere place or circumstance.

And even deprived of such reunions, there is still the telephone. The other day mine rang, and a dear voice came singing out of the past. A voice I hadn't heard in twelve years. "For goodness sake where are you?" I asked. "Come right on out."

"I'm afraid I can't," she laughed. "I'm still way down here in Texas. But I just suddenly got lonesome to talk to you."

And we found ourselves talking our heads off just as we used to do when she lived next door. And this has happened on other occasions with people too far away to see, but never too far away for real communication.

The same is true of city friendships. Neglect doesn't kill them; it simply deprives us of the happy hours that otherwise we might share. But even so robbed, our hearts remain filled with them, the consciousness of their devotion, their sincere interest in our concerns.

A teen-age girl going away to college for the first time expressed this very well: "If you don't miss me too much, Mother, I'll consider it a compliment. When you really love somebody you're so filled with them you're never too far apart."

THE FACE OF A FRIEND

You are among strangers. At a party perhaps, or in a press of people at a public function. And suddenly, out of all the meaningless, faceless faces, there blooms like a bright light—one!

It may be the face of a friend whom you see so frequently that —like the face of a husband, or your own features in a mirror—

you no longer really see it any more. Yet lifted from its familiar setting, suddenly it is new and clear to you and excitingly defined.

"Why, she's beautiful," you recognize in a burst of awareness. "I hadn't realized before how striking she is."

Or it may be someone whom you seldom see, but love. In this case too the face appears like an unexpected vision. The blood beats faster, the thrill of recognition is like that of finding a celebrity in your midst.

But better. Because the celebrity can give you no sense of identification. The celebrity will not call out to you in delight, nor can you call out to him. The celebrity furnishes no warm, welcome little island toward which you can draw in the choppy waters about you, and know that there you will be comfortable and safe. How lovely is the face of a friend!

MANY HANDS, LIGHT LABOR

IT's GOOD to be a woman when the friend who's offered to "get some of the guys from the office to come down and help" arrives at dawn one morning with the promised crew!

"Hey, I didn't expect you in the middle of the night," you hear your husband's astonished but glad protest. . . . And drifting blissfully back to sleep you are dimly aware of the hearty male voices kidding and conferring in and through the smell of perking coffee. Then the tramp of feet . . . the clank and bang and bump of rocks and lumber and hammers. Followed by the rhythmic chugging of a cement mixer borrowed from Frank, your dependable neighbor, whose old gray monster has coughed up concrete for almost every place on the Point.

When at last you arise from this seeming dream, they are hard at it. Figures crouch and measure at the balcony rail. One holds a ladder while a confederate saws away at the leafy branches of a tree. Others, stripped to the waist, are wrestling rocks at the sunny lake bank, where the walls need reinforcing. A duo are shoveling sand, mixing concrete, staggering under a loaded wheel-barrow, which they steer toward the patio.

All day, fortified by coffee, cold drinks, laughter, and comrade-ship, the activity continues. It is all you can do to persuade them to stop for a swim, a boat ride, a charcoal steak. At last, sweaty, grubby, but triumphant, they survey all they have achieved: The trees trimmed, the floats repaired, the bank more sturdy, the bal-cony sporting new rails, a beautiful new flagstone floor harden-ing on the patio overlooking the water—and they still don't want to quit!

"No, no, you've done enough—too much—it's a little miracle, all you've accomplished. And the work you've saved us—we'll never forget it—it's one of the nicest things that's ever happened to us."

You are all sitting around the long pine table on the porch now, refreshed from a swim, relaxed. The sun is going down in a golden glow behind the trees. A heron glides grandly across the sky and settles in the rushes. A coal oil lamp shines on the tired but still eager faces. There is the sweet earthy smell of woods and water, the first tentative tuning of the chorus of little night things.

"Ah, well, when you get a bunch of guys working together it goes fast and everybody enjoys it." A strong hand lifts a mug of coffee, eyes look thoughtfully into the still glowing and silvery dusk. "And after all, that's what got this country going. Take the first settlements, the house-raisings, the threshing parties—peo-ple helping each other."

WHAT PEOPLE DO TO US

HAVE YOU EVER WONDERED why most of us can be so many people? Not only in the mélange of personalities that quarrel in the privacy of our beings, but in our relationship to others.

A woman is one thing to her husband, often quite another to

her children. To one neighbor she may appear a regular Phyllis Diller; to the next someone as serious as Margaret Mead. The cop on the corner sees her as a trifle frumpy parent hastening duti-fully toward the school, while to the visiting executive who gives her a whirl at the club dance she's a creature so ravishing she ought to be on TV. She may represent half a dozen different versions of femininity, depending on the beholder.

And running the gamut of her contacts, without consciously contriving or even willing to do so, she finds herself enacting the role in which each one has cast her. For, curiously, different facets of our makeup are aroused by different personalities.

With some people we seem doomed to show off our worst fea-tures. One of my most admired and gracious relatives turns me into a blithering idiot. Never have I been in her presence that I didn't drop something, spill something, lose something, or say something stupid.

Another person to whom I am deeply indebted, and on whom I long to shower appreciation and praise, calls up instead some absurd and alarming demon determined only to shock and annoy her.

A certain couple to whom my husband and I are very close, are so prejudiced on some issues that they make both of us want to stand up and fight. Yet we feel that it would be rude to argue when they're guests at our house, and even more rude when we're guests at theirs. So we keep a cowardly silence, meanwhile fuming that these otherwise delightful friends can turn us into such simpering mealymouths.

Whether it's a matter of physical chemistry, or some secret disparity of the spirit, there are just some human beings with whom each of us can never hope to harmonize. People whom others enjoy, but who make us feel lackluster, and wanting in all charms. I used to consider such people a challenge, and deliber-ately sought their company in order to prove myself—and disprove nature.

I can tell you it was a waste of time. It's pointless to try to get in tune with people who don't give you the chance, when life abounds with others who inspire the gay, the good, the bountiful-best in you. Some friends touch the true and secret self on sight. These become your Best Friends. They are almost like your own blood (often they understand you better than your family). They see all the varied facets of your nature and package them into one human being who is precious to them. Just as you summarize their many attributes and hold them close to your heart.

FRIENDS ARE LIKE
BRACELET CHARMS

It was a party, in the truest sense of the word. An assortment of interesting people, small enough so that strangers could become acquainted, old friends could talk. Yet large enough to be full of laughter and music and pleasantries and stimulating new contacts.

On impulse I remarked to our hostess, Peg Howe: "You certainly have a lot of lovely friends."

"Oh, yes," she laughed. And lifting her braceleted arm she remarked, "My friends are the charms on my bracelet of life."

The charms! I thought. Why—yes. The enhancements, the adornments—that extra shining something. If you truly love and enjoy your friends they are a part of the golden circlet that makes life good.

When you gather them about you, you feel happy—and proud. Their accomplishments add a glow to your own being. What's more, you want to share them: "He's a distinguished surgeon, and his wife makes a home for all these foreign students—you must meet them." . . . "They both do little theater work, you'll just love them, they're both so alive—" . . . "He plays folk songs on the guitar and sings in three languages—" . . . "Now that the children are in school she's studying law." . . .

But not only their accomplishments, their qualities: "Helen is the most generous person I've ever known." . . . "Grace has the

most beautiful brown eyes—when she talks they just shine—" . . .
"Jim has a laugh that makes you feel good all over. And you can
depend on what he says, he'd never let you down—"

The person who can feel and speak this way about his friends
is truly blessed. His life is rich in meaningful relationships. His
"friends" are not a source of criticism and carping and jealousy
and gossip. They are people truly dear to him, so dear that he
can't refrain from singing their praises to others. And in so doing
he is always making new ones. For the way a person feels about
his friends is a pretty accurate indication of the kind of person he
or she is.

The man or woman who treasures his friends is usually solid
gold himself.

FINE STRANDS OF FRIENDSHIP

NEVER UNDERESTIMATE the deep attachments children form for
each other. They are meaningful and real. In their purity and
strength they are part of the sweet mystery of childhood, something that is seldom found in the later complexities of the adult
world.

Little girls are particularly prone to form these alliances. (Perhaps because the female of the species is created to be more
tender, more utterly giving of her emotions than the male?)
Little boys have best pals, but often their closest buddies are likewise their direst antagonists. They fight, verbally and physically.
And I have never known one to grieve deeply over the loss of such
a friend, either by moving away, a final smashup, or even death
itself.

When a very little girl has a best friend, however, she is likely
to worship her. They laugh, they whisper, they share secrets, they
go around with their arms about each other. They write each
other notes and think up surprises for each other. And when they
are forced to separate they are inconsolable.

Nancy was such a child in Texas; a dear little blonde with a bone disease. When we moved away our daughter was heartbroken. "What'll she do without me?" she wept. They corresponded for years and sent each other gifts and saved up Christmas money for phone calls.

Other mothers have witnessed this same manifestation. One showed me the touching postcards that her daughter's favorite small friend had mailed from every stop en route to California: "This is the first time I've ever been away from you. I'm crying so hard I can hardly see to rite."

Most of us outgrow such attachments, drifting apart emotionally and physically. If we meet in later life it's usually as strangers. Yet sometimes circumstances themselves are kind, and two who loved each other as youngsters cuddling dolls or swinging on a fence remain dear to each other throughout life.

Aunt Tressa was such a friend to my mother. She lived far away, but they never let the lovely strands of friendship fall apart. Every few years she would come to visit—small, dark, sparkling, with hands that could make a piano sprout wings and fly. And to hear them laughing and chattering away was to hear echoes of a far but never quite lost springtime when both were bubbling young.

Age could not change the essential spiritual communion they had with each other. A thing that children sense. For children, little girls especially, are close to nature, close to love. Instinctively they recognize that this joyful, unquestioning rapport with another human being is one of the most beautiful, significant things in life. That is why they rush headlong to claim it when it comes to them, and grieve for it so profoundly when it's gone.

Your Family—Your Cornerstone

Nothing is more important to human happiness than to be part of a fractious, forgiving, warm, tightly knit family.

—M.H.

THE FAMILY CORNERSTONE

THE ROAR of the cement mixer stops. The rocking, loud-mouthed monster gives a chugging sigh, as if to rest before spewing another thick gray load.

Your husband wipes his brow. The sunlight rippling on the water reflects on his face as he says, "Well, now we're ready to start the supporting columns. Say, this is kind of an event, at that, building our cabin. Maybe we ought to lay a cornerstone."

"Hey, yeah, how about it?" Your tall bronzed son turns from the pile of cinder blocks.

The little one, who's been busily "helping" by hauling little tin buckets of sand, demands, "What's a cornerstone?"

"Well, it's a kind of ceremony they have sometimes," you lamely attempt to explain. "When they put up public buildings, well like colleges or post offices or churches, sometimes they put souvenirs in the corner block. Say a coin or a newspaper, and their names."

"But what for?"

"Well, so that years later if the building's torn down, people will know who built it."

"But who'd ever want to tear our cabin down?"

"Help!" You turn to your grinning spouse.

"It's a kind of celebration, honey," he says—and instantly the word is taken up. "Hey, kids, c'mon, everybody, we're going to celebrate."

Already your daughter has dashed off to return triumphantly clutching assorted contributions—jacks, paper dolls, puzzles, the dog's collar.

"Oh, no, honey, not all that junk," her father groans.

Others with similar notions are weaned from the dramatic idea of burying treasure in the walls.

You settle for a new penny, the daily paper, a baby boot, and a tiny document gravely passed around and signed. All are stored in a cigar box, tied with a ribbon from the little girl's pigtail.

"Now we put it in the corner block—"

"Wait, wait, that picture I drew of the horse!" It seems so vital to the artist, a pause is arranged while the wobbly purple horse is likewise proudly interred.

"Now what?"

"Well, at this point they usually make speeches. If Mr. Ryland were here, he'd say a prayer. We'll just say a silent prayer in our hearts that we're glad we're all together and have come this far with our cabin, and hope we'll be able to finish it and be happy here."

Your husband deposits the box, applies the mortar. Together with his son, another cinder block is lifted into place.

"Now don't they hit it or something?" somebody pipes up. "With a bottle? I've seen pictures."

"Silly, that's only with ships. Besides, who's got any champagne? Though boy, oh boy, I could sure use some Hawaiian punch—"

"That's right, when do we eat? After all, it's no fun to celebrate unless you get something to eat."

"I'll see what I can scare up." You rise from your perch on a pile of lumber. You climb the rock steps. You see your family below you, silhouetted against the water—your quarreling, laughing, laboring family. And you think—that is what counts. This is what lasts when the rest of it is all over. Your family—your cornerstone.

"LISTEN," SAYS YOUR HEART

YOUR LITTLE BOY plunges onto your lap where you sit reading the paper, a warm damp bundle after his bath. Another child perches on the chair arm, still small boy enough to caress in a restless, hunting fashion.

"Read to us, Mother."

You put down your paper and take up the storybook. The rain pauses to rest as you sit there together. A golden-green light floods the sky, gilding the new featherings of the leaves outside the window, silvering the shingles of your neighbor's house, making a shining chariot of the family car parked in the drive.

Then the sky turns to rose, deepens to a rumbling purple, and the rain begins again, rhythmic and purposeful.

"Horsey! Camoool," the younger child interrupts the story now and then to point the pictures out. But mostly he lies relaxed, moist of chin, two fingers in his mouth.

His brother listens intently, palm cupping one cheek, or leaning down to clasp a pink heel and pick vaguely at his toes.

Their dad, in his robe, has heated up a cup of coffee and sits on the hassock at your feet, reading the paper you've discarded. "Hey!" he protests, as the younger child takes a sudden notion to crawl over your shoulder and snap off the light.

"Bad boy," scolds his brother. "Turn that right back on!"

"No, wait." You pull the baby back down. "This is cozy. It reminds me of when I was a little girl. My mother used to gather us all close like this, in a big chair in the dusk, and listen to the rain. . . . Listen—"

"Listen," whispers the older one. "Listen to it come down, boy, a regular cloudburst!"

"Listen to the lake," says your husband. "This keeps up it'll rise several inches by morning."

"Listen," the awed baby chimes in. His head is cocked. "I hear the fwowers."

Listen . . . listen . . . says your heart.

THE NEW CAR

YOUR HUSBAND calls one afternoon with that certain half-reluctant, half-reckless lilt in his voice that betokens surprise.

"Honey, you know how we've been worrying about that old car?"

"Yes?" you say eagerly, fingers crossed, letting him take the lead. "You think maybe we should get a new one?"

"Well, I've been looking. How'd you like to come help me pick one out?"

Through childhood's mysterious antennae the signal has already been flashed. "A car? New car!" They streak from all directions, big-eyed.

"Now not so fast, we're not sure yet."

You shove the vacuum into a closet and exchange your shorts for a skirt. "Now everybody wash up, but if you go along, no teasing. It's Daddy's money, remember, and his decision."

The old one seems suddenly dear and faithful when he drives up. You begin to fight an emotion that strikes whenever you've had to move, or a piece of furniture has to be replaced. An impulse half sentimental, half economic.

"I know." Your husband pats the dented hood. "She's taken us a lot of miles. And the engine's perfectly good."

The children emit a mass wail. "We are going to get a new one? You said—"

"Now nothing's decided yet. Be still."

Doubtful, but with rising anticipation, you are ushered into showrooms and begin your gingerly inspections.

"Now be careful of the seats, don't fingermark the glass—" . . . "Look, Mommy, a big shelf where I can have a doll bed—" . . . "Boy, push-button windows!" . . . "Man, oh man, I can't wait till I get my driver's license—"

Test rides are taken. Then, "I don't know. Which one do you like, honey?" your husband asks.

"She'll take the blue one," grins the salesman who long has served your family's needs. "I remember, your wife always wants blue."

"But the blue one hasn't got spinners," protests the thirteen-year-old. "Hey, Mister, you put on wheel spinners, no extra charge?"

The salesman laughs. "That kid's going to do all right. Sure, son, I think it can be arranged."

You drive home in the old one while minor adjustments are made. The kids keep the phone busy, too elated to eat. "Hey, we're getting a new car!"

He's still there when you return, this man who never seems to eat or sleep or have a life of his own apart from these shining vehicles. "Well, folks, hope you enjoy it."

"Pile in, everybody. Now, now—Mother's sitting up front with me."

"Dibs on this window." . . . "Dibs—dibs—" . . . "Hey, no fair, I said dibs first—"

"Now no fighting, and be careful of the upholstery."

"That's right, sit down, don't put your feet up, don't touch anything. Mom, look, he's already made a mark—"

Anxious, preening, vaguely guilty as you glimpse the old one standing abandoned and rather forlorn in the lot, you glide off. Smooth as a cloud it rides, quiet as a confidence.

"Let's take a ride, let's go to a drive-in, have some ice cream to celebrate."

You smile at your husband and at your young, sitting for this first rare period so quiet and pleased, almost too impressed to move. You know it can't last, this harmony, this newness, this sense of joy and value and beginning. But it's wonderful when it comes. You're glad you took the plunge.

You're glad you live in a land where it's possible for everyday people to go sailing down the highway in a snug house of glass and steel and power—a new car!

MY SISTER GWEN

JUST ABOUT the nicest thing I could wish for everybody is that they have a sister Gwen. My sister Gwen is gay, comical, friendly, exciting, dramatic, and beautiful. To be with her is to live with laughter; she is a fountain of sheer fun.

Her voice, though sweet, is rather loud; it rises in proportion to her enthusiasm. She would have made a good evangelist, for she is forever converting people—to clubs, causes, new hairdos, new decorating schemes, new interests and challenges. But she's as generous with her energies as her advice, joyously whacking out their slipcovers, papering their halls, dyeing their hair, teaching them to drive. Her visits strike with all the zest of an electric storm. The breeze of her personality rocks the house.

She is an insatiable sightseer. However often she has been to Washington, she must consume it afresh, right down to the rind. She loves the White House, swap shops, jewel collections, the Smithsonian, Congressional hearings, old bookstores.

On a recent stay she took in the White House twice to absorb the changes, engaging every guard in conversation, taking notes, pondering. Then off she rushed to comb secondhand stores for similar dusty treasures, donning jeans and a bright bandana to refinish them for us.

Tender and devoted to our mother, she is also the spark, the catalyst that keeps her active and spiritually young. "Now come on, Mama, it won't be any fun without you," she insists. And carrying her coat, and finding her a chair, she forestalls the fatigue of age.

She was determined that Mother see the John Glenn parade. "I'll pack a lunch and take a folding chair and we'll go early and get a good place." When rain made the plan unfeasible, she came up with an idea that would never have occurred to me. "The Congressional hearings! We can see him better there anyway." And sure enough, they sat directly behind all three of those first astronauts and came home glowing. My sister Gwen was especially elated, for she has made it a personal passion to learn everything possible about the space age.

She has a special technique of sightseeing with children, left over from rearing her own: "Always take along a jug of water and something to eat." This provender she stows in the car, portion-ing it out just before the mass assault on the Washington Monument or the F.B.I. "It's when they get hungry and thirsty that they get tired and cross. Also, a good stoking before you start means you don't waste time trying to find places to eat." They love to go with her, maybe because she's more interesting than anything they see!

Nothing's ever the same after my sister Gwen has gone. Your hair may be a different color, your house completely rearranged. But she's shined up your spirit along with the silver, hung rosy new curtains on the windows of your heart. You feel excited, exhilarated, revitalized.

WHEN A FAMILY FACES TROUBLE

THE TRUE TEST of a family is trouble. Will it be shattered by this grave blow, or will it survive to become even stronger than before?

Under the first impact it may stagger and falter, and for a brief appalling moment feel its own structure slipping, its very fate in doubt.

Then quickly the good family recovers, unites, feels itself somehow stronger than before. Qualities unsuspected in its own members come rushing to the fore: The ability to understand, to weigh and analyze a problem, and advise; the willingness to share each other's burdens, the capacity for sacrifice.

Members formerly at odds may be drawn together in the common cause of helping to overcome this thing which threatens the precious whole. Goodness and kindness cement the cracks, tighten the slipping bonds.

If a family can meet trouble together and triumph over it, then nothing can overcome that family. And each of its members will be able to cope with his own life a little better than before.

STARGAZING

"COME DOWN ON THE DOCK and look at the stars with me, Mother," the middle boy begs. "Let's go stargazing together."

"Oh, dear, it's so chilly," you hedge. "And it's getting kind of late."

"That's good, that's all the better. The later it is, the more stars. And we can take a blanket, you can put on a sweater."

"Oh, goodie, can I come too?" the littlest pleads, flinging down a toothbrush and grabbing for a robe.

"Not you. It's too cold," her brother protests.

"Oh, now, let's all go, shall we?" you urge. "After all, the sky's a big place, there are enough stars to go around."

Grudgingly the trip's proponent agrees. Trailing blankets and wraps you all grope down the rocky steps toward the float. The sky is blacker than it has been in weeks, the stars a fiery peppering. Some of them seem almost near enough to touch—the rungs of a shining ladder. They are more than reflected on the water, they are doubled and tripled in brilliance as the wind stirs, as if combing them through its black hair.

The broad wooden float is cool and damp as you cuddle down, Indian-fashion. The smaller ones creep inside the clumsy enfolding tent, nuzzling like ponies vying to be close. The older ones sprawl about, importantly citing constellations.

"I see the Big Dipper."

"Aaah, anybody can see that. I see Orion, the Big Bear, and Venus."

"I see the Three Bears and Goldilocks."

"There isn't any such constellation as that, is there, Mother? That's just a story."

"Well, I can still *see* it, can't I? You can see anything you want in the stars."

"That's right," you soothe. "That's how the constellations got their names in the first place. People who watched the stars thought they looked like pictures and made up stories to fit."

"It's still no fair, but tell us some more."

"Some people used to think the world was a huge room, and the sky a vast ceiling where the gods hung out the stars every night for lamps."

"Tell us some more. Tell us how you used to play out at night when you were a little girl."

And so you tell them—about Old Gray Wolf, and Redlight, and Run, Sheep, Run. "It was a small town, of course, and safe for children to play games under the stars. And we had this superstition—whenever we saw a shooting star we thought someone had just died, and we'd all get scared and run for home."

For some reason this strikes them as hysterically funny. But even as they are laughing, a streak of fire traces the sky.

"Hey, see that?" somebody gasps. "A shooting star!"

The laughter suddenly stops. They gaze at you, impressed. The little ones huddle closer. The bigger ones get to their feet.

"See what you started, Mom? I know it's silly, but—*beat you to the house!*"

IF MOTHER GOES TO JAIL

YOU'RE SITTING on the float one evening feeling benign toward the world. Above you perches the cabin achieved through faith, hope, and sheer togetherness. While your husband was wrestling boulders for the walls, you and the small fry were swinging pick and shovel.

The float itself was another family project. From it you've been diving, fishing, and chatting with people passing up and down the lake. "Nice place you have there," they call, these pleasant-looking men in the boat.

"Thank you," you beam. And are pleased as they cut the motor.

"Pull in," you invite. "My husband will be right back, I'm watching his lines for him."

They glance at the two rods and then at you. "Catch many?"

"They're not biting too well right now, but gee, I've sometimes brought in thirty or more. My husband only caught two tonight."

He comes loping down the steps and you present him. "Though I didn't catch your names," you say apologetically.

"Well—" They exchange glances. "We're the game wardens."

"All three?" you gasp.

"Yes, Ma'am. And we're checking on fishing licenses. You folks got licenses, I suppose?"

"You bet." Your husband digs for his wallet, which is gravely studied. "That's yours, how about your wife?"

"Who, me?" You feel astonished, acutely betrayed.

"She doesn't need one, does she?" your husband asks. "Why, she's the lousiest fisherman on the lake."

"I am not. Remember that time I caught—?" You gulp, look meek.

Patiently but grimly they explain. Yes, indeed. Out of state. Even property owning and paying taxes don't make no difference. 'Course if you were fishing from your own property, sitting on the bank . . .

But this *is* your property, you protest, and it's attached to the bank. Like that gambling ship they couldn't do anything about because of the gangplank, only this is legitimate.

"Lady, you can tell that to the judge." One of them is writing. Fixing you with a steely eye, he reads: "You are hereby charged with violating the fishing laws of the State of Virginia, and summoned to appear in court—"

You gape at him, heart pounding. He must be kidding! Such a nice young man. Surely he can't do this to you.

"Sign here." He really means it. Still astonished, you wonder what would happen if you refuse. But there are three of them, all huskies, against one paltry dame. Resisting arrest would hardly do.

"Listen, this is no fair!" you sputter, wanting to cry. "I'm a good wife and mother. I—I—tonight I wasn't even fishing."

"If you're on a dock with a fishline in sight, Ma'am, you're technically fishing. See you in court." They pull away.

The children come trooping down the bank. "Who was that? What happened?"

"Your mother just got arrested," their father laughs. "Listen, this should be fun. If you argue with the judge the way you can argue with me, I wouldn't bet a nickel on him."

"Well—it'll be an experience." You're beginning to see the possibilities. "And I've always wondered— Listen, will you treat me to a baby-sitter if I decide to go to jail?"

"Honey, I sure will."

"You really mean it, Mom? Oh, boy, wait'll I tell the guys!"

"Can I go stay with Gracie? And wear my new pink nightie? Can I tell my Sunday School teacher?"

"Think of the peace and quiet. I'll take my typewriter along and write a protest. I'll write a book. And let's face it—any woman who's been raising a flock of children would enjoy a few days off, even if she has to spend them in jail!"

COVER THE CHILDREN, IT'S COLD

THE COLD is a great animal that bestirs itself by night and prowls the earth, blowing its chill breath through the walls of your country cabin. You feel it first against your face, your nose, and burrow instinctively deeper into the nest. Then responsibility, as subtle but as strong, intrudes: The children. . . . No, no, they're perfectly all right, if not they'll call you . . . But you cannot escape the nagging of that second beast, conscience. Children, it insists, never really *know* if they're cold.

It routs you at last. In sleepy protest you crawl out, go padding across the chilly floors.

The fire has almost died out. Only embers light the rustic room. Shivering, you stir the coals, pile on another log. Then you go digging into closets for more blankets and those odds and ends that can be made to serve where it is dark and style means nothing; where there is no motive except to combat that primitive adversary, cold.

From bunk to bunk you proceed. The children lie huddled into nature's own position of protection, curled up like hibernating cubs embracing themselves against the cold. Gently you unwind them, pile on the additional bedding. And as they groan against your ministrations, you insist, "Call me if you need any more, it's cold."

The mission completed, you go back to see about the fire. The logs lie sullen, refusing, beyond a scant fume of smoke, to cooperate. Kneeling, you bait them with papers, which instantly spring into a joyous flame. You break fresh kindling across your knees and thrust that too beneath their stubborn weight. There is a welcome crackling. The room is rosy now with leaping light. Even the big logs want to get in on the party. Grumbling at first, then enthusiastic, they catch, begin to burn. And it is so suddenly pleasant, so merry, this fire in the lonely night, that you long to make a pot of coffee, to sit by it and just enjoy it for a while.

But you know that despite its splendor and show of strength, it will prove no match for the antagonist outdoors. For he has summoned up the wind to join his forces; the wind is shouting taunts and battering mightily at the windows. So you too must call up allies. You go about flicking on heaters that begin to sing softly and play their own rosy glow across the floors.

You stand a moment more, soaking up the warmth, reluctant to leave. Then you go plunging back to your own nest, pull up the covers. Let the contest continue—the brash wind blow, the hearth fires answer. All your babes are snug now, safe, protected, and you can sleep in peace.

THE MERRY-GO-ROUND

YOU COME UPON IT unexpectedly as you drive through the little town. A park with picnic tables. A pool. A few booths with their games of chance. And oh, the magic circle turning with its necklace of colored lights—a merry-go-round.

You consult your husband as the clamoring of the children begins. You know their fate hangs in balance as adult considerations are weighed: Should you stop, can you spare the time? Your suspense is almost as great as theirs. However, you assure him, "It's all right if you don't think we should."

A childlike relief surges up within you as he pulls up by the side of the road. "C'mon, everybody out that wants to ride the merry-go-round."

You walk across the trampled grass with its nostalgic memories. Up to the little booth. "How many?" (How many tickets to enchantment? How many cardboard stubs to touch the stars?)

"You take them on it," you urge. "I'll hold the baby."

"Me too, me too!" The child reaches out to the spinning loveliness, trying to grasp its essence as he strives to touch and taste the moon.

"No, darling. When you're older. See, we'll watch Daddy and the others ride."

It is slowing, the chipper metallic tinkling of the music is slowing down. People surge forward, and this too you remember—the frightful anxiety as they rush to catch a horse.

The rearing black one with bulging eyes—no, taken.

The low-diving sorrel with the silver tail—it too is gone.

Help them, oh help them to find and capture the ones they want!

Ah—you sigh, for they are all together: the boys—one casual and rather clumsy as he clambers on, too big for this kind of thing, his manner firmly announces; the younger with his shining eyes and tousled hair; the ecstatic little girl.

The child in your arms watches, transfixed. His wave is almost automatic. He is pondering this mysterious revolving toy. What is it?

What is the secret of its rapture, this melodious plunging up and down? These colored lights like fruits that you cannot touch or taste—what do they mean?

And you too ponder as you watch it work its wonder on the faces all about—other parents who stand watching blissful children spiral past on flying steeds. Is it that all life is a mystery and a marvel, hurling you now high, now low, but forward, if only in a circle that echoes the revolving of the globe?

You don't know, you cannot say. Only that a child on a merry-go-round has captured Pegasus himself and soars above the world.

THE SWING

WHAT CAN EQUAL the joy of an old-fashioned rope swing?

To a child it is at once his homely friend and his most royal possession, gracing his castle yard like a throne. In mellow dignity it occupies its chosen place, the ground beneath the firm board seat worn bare, leaves and stirring boughs and sky its wondrous canopy.

It is the focal point for gatherings and games. It is the king's chair, to be conquered, abdicated, or occupied in soaring majesty. It is a place of refuge when the child is lonely or hurt.

A swing, to assume its true and rightful identity, must hang alone. It shouldn't be part of a playground set strung up on bars along with seesaws and rings. It can't be one of half a dozen in a park—public, impersonal, chained to iron posts. It has to belong to someone who loves it. Its strong rope fists must grip bark. It must claim its special tree.

An old-fashioned rope swing is usually hung by a father who remembers the swings of his own childhood. He chooses the toughest coil of rope he can find and a sturdy board to be notched with a jackknife for the seat. The hanging is gaily and noisily accomplished, with youngsters laughing and yelling directions and bouncing with impatience, thick as blackbirds.

An old-fashioned rope swing is something to be shared. Everyone must try it, even Mother and Dad and aunts and uncles. Children come running from blocks around to take turns in it, fight over it, beg to be pushed in it, to be "run under," and know the glory of the world's dipping and their feet rattling the leaves.

A rope swing is fun to pump in, standing up singly or by twos. It's fun to climb hand over hand, and to slide down, palms burning. It's fun to wind up and spin in. And its seat is a pleasant place to lean on, to dreamily watch the lazy glide of the ground below.

A swing is the instrument of a child's imagination—a ship's rigging, a circus trapeze, a rocket to the moon . . . Its song is made up of rope creak and leaf rustle and birds twittering . . .

A rope swing is like a blessed presence that is taken for granted. And when something happens to it, when the seat breaks or the rope frays away, or a child rushes out after a rain to find that it has shrunk foolishly high, he feels a sense of shock and loss. Almost of betrayal; there is a loneliness about it, akin to that when Mother is sick or gone.

Children often fight over such a swing, sometimes fall out of it, or are hit by it. That too is part of its nature, that makes it almost a human thing. The tears and bruises and parents scolding. As if the swing were giving a small preview of the eternal marvel and the peril of life.

Rooted in earth, but headed for heaven. A wonderful thing, a swing!

THE FRAGILE BALL

ON A GLORIOUS GOLDEN SUNDAY the older children cavort with their wives and sweethearts and friends on the dock. You hear the music of their voices, their laughter, their playful tormenting. "Another crack like that and I'll throw you in."

"I dare you!"

At a tremendous splash the little ones prance about in delight, begging, "Me, me, throw me!" Vainly above the skidding commotion you yell for them to stop, it's dangerous, now quit.

The boys are young and brown and rippling with muscles, the girls slim-legged in their vivid suits. Turquoise, tangerine, emerald, and strong primary colors, yellow, ruby red. All these weave their patterns against the steel-blue water and the vibrant blue of the wet dock.

Your husband has bought a beach ball that is transparent, a globe of sheer dazzling pink, through which the sun shines as they toss it, playing "Keep away." It bounces on the water and the Dalmation dives after it, nosing it ahead of her frantically, for the airy globe is not to be caught.

"Watch out, if she gets a tooth in it she'll break it."

"She can't, it's too slippery." A young body slices into the water, snatches it away from the pursuing snout; then together boy and dog wrestle in a wild splashing that sends a fountain of fire into the air.

Inner tubes, glossy black circles, lie about. Orange life jackets hang from posts. The red and white boat rocks beside the pier. On a rock one boy stands fishing, calm and detached from the noisy merriment, his line a delicate tracing as he casts.

Another boy is intent on skipping stones. He chooses flat ones, and leaning slightly back pitches them across the glossy expanse. "Sssspt! Sssspt!" comes the sound as the stone kisses the water and leaps forward toward new lips. Bracelets of silver follow its course; swift, bright, spreading and blending they multiply.

Boats go by, making huge waves which come rolling, glassy-backed. The float bangs and rocks, throwing people off balance, making the young ones cry out, "These are great, come on, dive in." They plunge into the heaving water, and with each contact, as with the stones, there is a mad new multiplication of light.

The fiery patterns are infinite—and moving on into infinity. They are elusive and not to be caught by the wondering eye.

They are like the bright pink ball that flies at the touch of the fingers and cannot be held except in destruction and collapse.

They are like youth and love . . . They are like life.

THE LETTER HOME

ALL OVER THE WORLD tonight women sit writing: The brides, still a trifle self-conscious as they perform this new domestic task; the wives so long married it has become second nature—writing the letter home.

"Dear Mother and Dad— Well, we made it! It was a long hard trip, but so wonderful I want to tell you all about it. Jim was so sweet. No girl ever had a lovelier honeymoon."

Or, "Dear folks: I'll try to snatch a little time while the baby's napping, to report on what's been happening." Or, "Dear Families—including Margaret and Elmer, Grandpa and Grandma, Bob and Uncle Mac: Please forgive me for the carbon copies. Have been so frantically busy that the only way to catch up on our correspondence is to write to everybody at once."

And typed or handwritten, on finest stationery or the back of a child's wobbly drawing, they have a quality all their own—a woman's letters home.

For she has left her own people to follow her man. And whether they have moved just a few hundred miles away or across a continent, an ocean, her letters trace the course of her new life. A life filled with all the incidents, great and small, that go into the fabric of a family: The first tooth and the first operation. The raise in salary, the Couples' Club they've joined, the church, the grocery store, the neighbors. The hopes, the prospects, the aspirations; and often—though these are touched on lightly, if mentioned at all—the disappointments and worries.

For slowly, subtly, a woman senses that this is a record of happiness, actually, her letter home. Not that she is expected to write only of sunshine and roses. Nor that she's too proud to complain. No, it's something deeper, more significant. A gradual recognition that, however she may put it off, a wonderful thing happens when she sits down to write that letter home.

For this is her journal, her account. And strangely, it is the good, the gay, the funny things that come swimming to the surface of the chaos of raising a family. By a kind of magic, in the sheer act of recollecting and recounting, her own appreciation takes over, her confidence in the future, her gratefulness. Seldom does she consciously think: "I won't write that. It would worry them." Rather, the problem doesn't seem so bad in retrospect— and less interesting than Sue's first formal and Ted's paper route.

Her words are awaited hopefully all over the world, on farms, in cities, in little towns. No author, however famous, has an audience more eager, more faithful. Day after day, parents watch for the letters, fret when they don't arrive, wondering what's wrong. And oh, the rejoicing, the lift of the spirits when they do. "Here it is. Well, it's about time! Let's see what Alice has to say."

So women sit writing. Up and down the street, in the big cities and the small towns, all over the world. Writing that diary of their destiny, making their entry into the account books of their lives: "Dear Folks . . ." "Dear Mother and Dad . . ."

MOTHER, I'M HOME!

"MOTHER, where are you? I'm home!" Day after day you hear that call. Over and over. When the littlest bounces in from kindergarten, proudly bearing his crayon drawing: "Mommy, here I am. Look what I made today. Mommy, I'm home!" At three o'clock when the older ones begin to streak in: "Hey, I'm home." Sometimes on weekends or holidays, the ones away at college. "I'm here! It's me. I'm home."

And with that cry come both responsibility and rejoicing. As life begins to surge through the house you take up the tasks it brings. The sandwiches they demand before tearing off for football practice, the money for Cub Scout dues, the things to be found: "Honey, those shoes are right under the bed where you left them." The phone calls: "Mary wonders if Jeanie can stay awhile."

And the day's adventures to be listened to, its triumphs and its disasters: "I made it, I made it. I'm a cheerleader!" "Mom, Miss Johnson promised I could wash the board, but she chose Marie." "Mother, I've just got to talk to you about this boy."

It's a signal that peace is ended, that cry "I'm home." With the banging of the door, your day is stirred once again to action. No longer are you your own person. You belong to them.

Yet, in the confidence of that cry, you feel a surge of pride. They want you; they seek you out. However poorly equipped you may feel for the job at hand, at least you're available and willing, and to them you're invaluable.

"Mother, I'm home!" Oh, the ego in that announcement. Oh, the glorious awareness of love. "How important I am," it seems to say, and you laugh sometimes at its brashness. But your heart is tender too, even as you realize that they take you for granted— the fact of your presence and your delight in *their* presence.

"I'm home." They rap softly on your door at night, tiptoe in.

"You can go to sleep now, Mother. I'm home." And oh, the relief of that voice, the comfort of that good night kiss, for the long vigil is ended, the hours of worrying. They're safe; the last one's in.

They grow up so fast; they go away one by one. After a while only on their visits does that glad cry come. Hectic visits, filled with their outside concerns—dates, parties, or the turmoil of families of their own. The cribs are put up, the high chairs produced, and you know that you are no longer the center and hub of their existence, no matter how joyously they proclaim their own home-coming, bursting in. Home is somewhere else. A different job, a different life, a different love to follow yours, a different person to greet them when they return.

And that once-familiar cry has taken on a new significance. It means that you don't have to watch the clock any more when they're late. You don't have to worry. They have reached their destination. Each one is safely in. In a new and much more wonderful way, each voice is assuring you: "I'm home, Mother. I'm *home!*"

A Woman and Her Faith

The Lord is my shepherd; I shall not want—

— *The Twenty-third Psalm*

A FIRM FOUNDATION

LUCKY IS THE WOMAN who can come to her marriage with her faith intact, and her will to practice it strong. And lucky is her child. For, often with her husband, sometimes single-handed, she provides what every child needs most: Order. Structure. A sense of being sheltered by forces older, stronger, and sounder than himself.

She equips her children, from their earliest memories, with the greatest weapon, consolation, and aid they will ever have—prayer. "Bedtime, now let's say our prayers." . . . "Timmy, you can give the blessing." . . . "Don't worry about the exam, honey, ask God to help you—and I'll say a little prayer." This amulet against danger and evil, this comfort in times of disappointment, this touchstone of hope. Nothing else that she could give them by way of luxuries or attention could last so long or help them more. Deep in their beings she is embedding a power that they will never be without, no matter how old they grow or how far they stray from her principles and beliefs.

And all about her family the woman of religious convictions rears the rafters of her faith, roofs it with her love of God, and furnishes it with the activities of worship, organized and otherwise, and ushers her dear ones in. Her church is often an adjunct of home, which children embrace, accept, or reject, according to individual age, nature, or stage. For youngsters go through many phases:

The first excitement of Sunday School with its flannel board stories and little red chairs ("Jesus Loves Me, This I Know!" . . .). The mystic ardors of adolescence when they may yearn to go into convents, become missionaries, or study for the ministry . . . The often searing and turbulent times when they begin to kick at the very structure that has given them shelter. ("How do we know? You can't prove anything by the Bible.")

This period can be painful. The other day a friend told me, "Bill's reached the age where they stop picking on God and start picking on you." As I looked puzzled—"You know, they almost all go through it. When they decide they're atheists. Since there's no God to blame for things any more they've got to blame somebody, so they blame Mother. The world is all your fault." This hurts. But after a child or two, the woman whose faith is strong knows that "this too shall pass." While stubbornly, proudly, even merrily, she and her stand survive.

And this too is her priceless gift: She will not be moved. She will listen to their logic, she will agree where agreement is just. But basically her faith holds fast. It has sustained her through all the storms of family living, and it will sustain her now. And even as they challenge and scorn it, children are glad that she will not give in. Bigoted, old fashioned, narrow-minded—yes, they may call her all these things (or think them). Yet she inspires awe as well as exasperation. She believes in something.

She is someone they know and trust and respect—and she believes. She is no stranger to the cruelties and injustices of life— and she believes. While others flounder and grope for answers— Mother believes. In a world where so little else is stable, this is no small thing.

So there she stands, in the old-fashioned house of her faith. So patient, so small and yet so mighty, holding the lamp of her love for him. In all the shifting, foundering world, the child knows that this one thing will not change. He can turn toward it whenever he's ready. He can come home.

FAITH IS A PRIVATE AFFAIR

IT TAKES YEARS, often a lifetime, to reach one's religious convictions, or at least a workable philosophy to live by.

It takes trial and error, despair, and even bitter rejection as you follow false paths, find yourself at dead ends, and retreat, rest, and wait. Then a new spark is touched in you—by something someone says, an example, a demonstration, another book (of the many, many books you've read), and off you go again. But each time a little more secure, less likely to grope and grapple in vain.

What eventually evolves may be a special combination of principles, precepts, and convictions that has never met in anyone else before—and that can't be transferred to another. Yet if it enhances your joy in living, makes you a better person, and sustains you in times of trouble, that is the test.

I don't think anyone is truly happy until he has worked out some private pattern, not only for getting along with people but for getting along with God.

MOM, I COULD HEAR MY HEART

DIALOGUE with a young philosopher . . .

"Mom, I could hear my heart beating against my pillow last night. It was thumping away so loud it almost scared me."

"We all hear our hearts beating that way sometimes."

"Y'know, it's funny we don't hear it more often. I mean it's funny that we've got all this junk inside of us, all this machinery going and we can't hear it at all."

"Well, we're pretty well insulated—all that flesh and skin."

"Yeah, but it's still funny. The lungs breathing and the heart pumping and all that blood rushing around. And the stomach working away at your food, and all those valves and whatever they are opening and closing and so busy—it's like a factory, it still seems like we could hear it."

"Yes, I guess it does."

"When people make things you can hear them. Factories make a lot of noise. Motors make noise. Trains, airplanes, ships—nearly everything that people make makes noise."

"That's right. Even watches tick."

"But hardly anything that God makes makes noise."

"How about animals?"

"Sure, they growl and all that, but that's only when they're mad or hungry. That's their speech; the machinery part of them is just as quiet as ours. And the trees are quiet except for the wind. And grass and flowers and butterflies and birds and worms and spiders —why, just about everything else you can think of is quiet."

"That's right—the sun's quiet, and so is the moon. Except for the wind and rainstorms just about everything in nature is still. I'd never thought of it before."

"Neither had I, but it's true. And I thought of it!" He regards you for a moment of shining silence. "You know it's pretty exciting to think of something nobody else has ever thought of maybe. I mean nobody else in the whole world."

"Even thoughts must come from somewhere," you remark.

"Yeah. So they must come from God. Maybe thoughts are the most important of all the silent things God makes. And it makes you feel wonderful when He sends a really good one straight to you."

MOTHERS ARE SELDOM ATHEISTS

MEN say there are no atheists in foxholes. Women can testify that there are no atheists in delivery rooms.

For never is a woman so close to her creator as when she is giving birth. Never is she so at the behest of forces beyond herself, nor so in league with life. And when she hears her baby cry, or holds it for the first time in her arms, she knows that she has been party to a miracle.

A woman doesn't waste much time quibbling about God in moments of family crisis, either. I doubt if there are many atheists in ambulances rushing an injured son to a hospital (or a husband who's just had a heart attack) . . . Or awaiting a doctor's pronouncement outside an operating room . . . Or just watching for the blessed swing of light into the driveway late at night, signaling that a daughter is safely home.

A MINISTER'S TRUE ACHIEVEMENT

THIS DOESN'T APPLY to all ministers, fortunately, and certainly not ours. But I've often wondered why some ministers, in relating their successes, so often speak of material things: Of mortgages reduced or paid off altogether, of new buildings, or old ones impressively improved. Sometimes I've even heard them refer to the physical framework in which they function (the church itself, the parish hall, and whatever other adjuncts that accompany it) as a "plant."

A plant! Acceptable jargon to the pros of the cloth, no doubt; but to the layman—well, it has a cold and clanging sound. Smacking somehow of assembly line efficiency—of canning souls in mass production.

Conscientious ministers, even more than some doctors, are on call at any hour of day or night, seven days a week. Their personal responsibilities and sacrifices are monumental. How sad then that pride or modesty or maybe some people's sensitivity prevents them from acknowledging their true achievements: "We succeeded in comforting and helping so many. We healed the sick and aided the poor. We brought hundreds of people into a closer relationship with God."

THE AFTERGLOW MEANS HOPE

MY MOTHER always loved sunsets. This is true of many people, but Mother had a special feeling for them; she kept almost daily appointment with them, and she savored them until the last glow faded from the sky.

We lived in a small Iowa town which boasts a long and lovely lake. And though our house was small, it overlooked a tag-end of the water where the sun seemed to fling its gaudiest banners at the end of the day.

"Oh, just look at that sunset!" Mother was always urging. "You can do those dishes later—your lessons can wait." We must stop whatever we were doing to follow her pleased gaze upward. "Isn't that the most beautiful sky you've ever seen?"

She always acted as if a sunset were something new and glorious and amazing, and we must observe it with as much intensity as if no sunset were ever to appear again. And though we often teased her about it, I realize now that those flaming sunsets compensated for many things we lacked during those grim depression years. They were her daily luxury.

Later when the bright hues had melted into the dusk and there was nothing left of the sunset but a last lingering band of burning rose, she would return to the porch a minute and stand there, arms wrapped in her apron sometimes against the chill, and murmur: "The afterglow means hope."

Hope. The afterglow means—hope! . . . The boy of your dreams would call . . . The test grade would be high . . . You'd get that scholarship for college . . . The job you wanted so desperately would materialize . . . The great big wonderful world of love and wealth and achievement would open up to you . . . For these are the faces of hope when you are young and looking up, eagerly seeking answers in a band of final color across a darkening sky.

As for her. Dimly I sensed the meaning of hope to my mother: The problems of all those about her would be resolved. Wounds would be healed, family frictions smoothed . . . The doctor's report on Dad would be favorable . . . The company policy would be more generous. There would be enough money to go around . . . Her children's often turbulent lives would get straightened out—the boys would find themselves, the girls would marry the right sweethearts—in time they would all be happy, make good.

For while the hooks upon which a youngster hangs his hopes are intensely selfish and personal, those of a mother are multiple; they encompass the entire circle of her family. Her dreams are no longer rooted in self, but in these others.

Yet standing on that porch together long ago, each of us saw in that smoldering band of light a symbol of happier, brighter tomorrows.

Hope. "The afterglow means hope." I don't know whether she had heard the phrase or coined it out of her own indomitable spirit. But I think of it whenever I see the quiet rosy afterlight that follows the blazing sunset. As if a few stubborn coals remain against the coming darkness, little fires of faith that cling long after the sunset is gone.

A BUSY MOTHER'S PRAYER

DEAR LORD—

You know it isn't that I don't have enough love to go around. It's just that there are so many of them, and my time and strength won't stretch that far.

Today, for instance, I was so busy coaching Bill on English that I couldn't go along with Jeanie to dancing school. She's having trouble with that new step for the recital, too; she wanted me to watch.

But if Bill doesn't pass this special English course he won't get into college. And you know how important that is, especially after losing that time in the service. Yet Jeanie looked so pathetic going off alone with her little suitcase that I felt guilty . . .

And their dad. So often I forget to do the little things he asks me to. I didn't save those clippings. I let the kids get into his tackle box. I'm sometimes so preoccupied in the morning I'm not even sure whether or not I've kissed him good-by. This isn't right.

A man needs a good send-off to face the day quite as much as the youngsters do . . .

Choices—all these choices! Between being a den mother for Tommy or a Girl Scout leader for Ruth. Between all the conflicts of music lessons and dental appointments and birthday parties and homework and just plain talking with them seven days a week, sometimes far into the night. No woman can possibly keep up with it all, no matter how hard she tries. Somebody's bound to feel neglected, to think, even if he never says so, "You don't love me as much—"

But you know it isn't any lack of love. It's only lack of energy, of strength, of time. So give me a little extra, please, if possible. And while you're at it, patience, so that I don't get cross and make the problem worse.

Amen.

(And oh, yes, if you could possibly work in an hour or two of peace and quiet and rest for me I'd be so grateful. In fact, it would help all of us a lot!)

SO POOR, SO RICH

DIALOGUE with a colored cabdriver:

"There were twelve of us children and we were very poor, only our mother taught us to be rich. 'What d'you mean poor?' she'd say whenever we'd complain. 'Your father gave you two good eyes to see with, and two good hands to work with, and two good feet that'll carry you wherever you want to go. That's being rich, son, that's being rich.

" 'There are plenty of people that can't see—you can use your eyes to help them, that's how rich you are.

" 'There are some people that can't even walk—you can walk to them and lift them up. Some people have to bear the burdens in this life and some people have to be carried. You be the person that learns to do the carrying. You be the strong—that's what really counts, that's what makes you rich . . .'

"Mother was a gentle-spoken woman. I never heard her use rough language, and neither did any of her six sons. 'A person is judged,' she always told us, 'by what comes out of his mouth.'

"And she always had an answer for everything. When my sister would say, 'It don't pay to be good, Mama—look at our neighbor, what a wonderful woman she was, and she's dead. And how some of the worst people just live on and on,' my mother would say: 'If you had company for dinner what flower would you pick for the table? Wouldn't you go into the garden and pick the best? That's the way it is with the Lord—he don't want the old bad ones. No, no, he says, let them be, maybe if I give 'em some more time they'll improve. But I want the loveliest, the nicest, the best—even little babies sometimes.'

"My mother didn't need Thanksgiving to remind her to be grateful. She was grateful every day of her life for her husband and her church and her children, and for living in a country where everybody can be free. And if he looks at it right, he can be rich!"

"WE'LL COME"

IT SEEMS such a pity that the scattered members of families almost never get together except in times of loss.

Someone dies. Someone dearly beloved. And suddenly the telegrams and letters begin to fly, the phone calls are being made. People who correspond only at Christmas now send wires, special deliveries. People who haven't heard each other's voices in months, even years, are communicating: "Oh, no! I'm so sorry— when did it happen? We'll come. We want to come." . . .

We'll come. We want to come . . . Suddenly it seems imperative. It is a compelling desire. For the news that has summoned us in the cause of sorrow has warm and quite wonderful overtones. We must go, we must draw together in this hour when one of our own has passed. We want to, for the sake of that person, but also for our own. To comfort and support each other. And oh, to see each other again—brothers and sisters long apart. Aunts and uncles and cousins. Yes, and second cousins, too. The whole clan.

So many of them, arriving so unexpectedly from so many places. It is a revelation, sweet and rather startling. Not only that they are so numerous, but that they too should want to come. And that in this busy world where distances are great and relatives tend to become strangers, blood ties still are strong.

How good it is to see them. How consoling. And despite the sadness of the occasion, how pleasant in so many ways. The visits so solemnly begun drift off into laughter and good talk: "I hadn't realized you had so many children. That makes me a great aunt, doesn't it? And they're so pretty—whose side do they take after, ours or Mac's?" . . . "Now let's see, whatever became of Lou's girl, Irene?" . . . "Remember the time Dad spanked all of us for going swimming that day the waves were so big?"

Reminiscences. The matching of statistics. News. And the old family friends who are so much a part of the past that they too belong: "Your papa came running to our house the night you were born." . . . "Your mother and I went to school together—" The family doctor who saw you all through so many illnesses is there. The neighbors from the old house on Seneca Street.

They too wanted to come. Out of respect to the one who is gone, yes, that is their excuse. But mainly to claim their own memories of the lost days once again, days in which he played a part, the precious days that are past.

And as you all sit around laughing, talking, eating the food the neighbors have brought in, you remark: "How Dad would have enjoyed this. Oh, how happy he would have been to be with all of us." And you add, "If only people could have get-togethers like this when we're all alive!" And everyone agrees.

But we can't. This too we acknowledge. We are so busy, so far apart. It takes the deep seriousness of death to draw us, to make us realize that all lives that relate to us are dear—these scattered lives. And when it is all over, though you rejoice at having claimed them once more, it is sad to say good-by. Then a dear little woman, strong in faith, says simply: "We'll meet again. Don't worry, it's all right. We'll all meet again."

Again something warm and wonderful comes over you. You realize, "Why, yes, that's right. He'll be there too—and we'll all be together again!"